The Descendants
of
Joseph Devor
of
Path Valley
Pennsylvania

Anna Hawley Grosvenor

Heritage Books
2025

HERITAGE BOOKS
AN IMPRINT OF HERITAGE BOOKS, INC.

Books, CDs, and more—Worldwide

For our listing of thousands of titles see our website
at
www.HeritageBooks.com

A Facsimile Reprint
Published 2025 by
HERITAGE BOOKS, INC.
Publishing Division
5810 Ruatan Street
Berwyn Heights, MD 20740

International Standard Book Number
Paperbound: 978-0-7884-1213-4

DEDICATION

I certainly owe a lot of thanks to a lot of folks who have helped over the years to accumulate the contents of this book. I must especially thank my husband, Richard Grosvenor, who has encouraged and helped me with the compiling of this book.

My daughter, Dorothy Grosvenor, has encouraged me and has also helped as a proof reader.

My mother, Carrie Devor Hawley, helped by making me acquainted with many of our relatives beginning when I was but a little child.

There are many cousins, aunts and uncles who have contributed to this knowledge over the years. I hesitate to begin to list them on this page, but they will show up in their proper places in the book. Many of them are now gone, but I loved them all.

I dedicate this book to all of them.

THE DESCENDANTS OF JOSEPH DEVOR
OF PATH VALLEY, PENNSYLVANIA

C O N T E N T S

Chapter I   Joseph Daver/Deavor/Devor..................1
and His Children's Families

Chapter II   Descendants of James Devor...............9
Hannah's Descendants.....................11
Joseph's Descendants 12
Jemima's Descendants.....................13
John's Descendants.......................13
Rolland's Descendants....................18
James's Descendants......................21
Richard M/E Descendants..................22
Lydia's Descendants......................26

Chapter III   Descendants of Jesse Daver/Deavor.......27
Jane's Descendants.......................29
Mary's Descendants.......................34
Joseph's Descendants.....................47
James's Descendants......................48
David's Descendants......................48
Jacob's Descendants......................65
Amos's Descendants.......................94

Chapter IV   Descendants of Jacob Deavor.............97
Martha's Descendants.....................99
James's Descendants.....................104
Annie's Descendants.....................105
Adam's Descendants......................106
Hannah's Descendants....................110

SOURCES   Each of the Sources is followed by
a name in parentheses that identifies
the author...............................111

INDEX   Lists all the names in the book........113

THE DESCENDANTS OF JOSEPH DEVOR
OF PATH VALLEY, PENNSYLVANIA

INTRODUCTION

Joseph Daver, a native of Scotland, migrated to Chester County, PA where in 1781 he was taxed for 100 acres. After the death of his wife, about 1790, he moved to Path Valley and lived near Spring Run. Path Valley is a pleasant spot in Franklin County in South Central Pennsylvania. The Valley is east of the Tuscarora Mountain and is 22 miles long and from 1.5 to 3 miles wide. The first settlers of Path Valley were Scotch-Irish, some of whom came as early as 1748.

Joseph spelled his name Daver or Deavor. His oldest son James spelled it Devor. All of James descendants also spelled it Devor.

Joseph's second son, Jesse, used his father's spelling. He signed his Will Jesse Daver, but Deavor is on his tombstone. Jesse's children changed the spelling of their name to Devor.

Joseph's third son, Jacob, used the Deavor spelling and his descendants still do.

William Tecumseh Sherman Deavor, who wrote the first authoritative book on the Devors used the Deavor spelling for all the descendants of Jacob. W.T.S. Deavor's book "A BRIEF HISTORY OF THE DEAVOR FAMILY IN AMERICA" (1896) has been updated in the book by Betty M. Mann, "DEVORE/DE VORE FAMILIES 1500-1992." More information has been provided on ancestors who were only briefly mentioned by W.T.S. Deavor or who were left out because of the difficulty of research in the late 19th Century. When there is a conflict between these two books, the DEVORE/DE VORE book has been followed.

Additional Devor information has been provided by relatives of the author, some of whom have made genealogy a serious hobby. Corwin Johnston, in 30 years of research, brought the Devor history down to 1948. His manuscript was not published and was not available for inclusion in the DEVORE/DE VORE book.

Other Devor relatives have brought the Devor history down to the present day.

A few words about the numbering of the people in this book. The numbers start at " 1 " in each chapter with the first person in that chapter.

A plus sign (+) in front of the number means that person is listed later in the chapter with more descendants.

THE DESCENDANTS OF JOSEPH DEVOR
OF PATH VALLEY, PENNSYLVANIA

FIRST GENERATION

Joseph DAVER/DEAVOR/DEVOR, b. ca 1745 in Scotland; d. 26 Apr 1824, Spring Run, Franklin Co., PA; bur. Spring Run, Franklin Co., PA.

Joseph DAVER was enrolled as a Private, 1st Class in Captain John Craig's 6th Company, 3rd Battalion, Chester County Militia, according to the evidence of a Company Return dated July 1, 1789.

In his "Brief History of the Deavor Family in America" William T.S. Deavor spells his ancestor's name either Daver or Deavor. Later the name became commonly spelled Devor.

Joseph DAVER/DEAVOR m. (1) Miss (_____) before 1765.

Children:
+   2 M   i   James DEVOR
+   3 M   ii   Jesse DAVER
+   4 M   iii Jacob DEAVOR
+   5 F   iv   Esther DEVOR
     6 F   v   Eleanor (or Ellen) DEVOR, b. ca 1770, Chester, PA. She m. (1) Joseph HOLLINGSWORTH. Children were Jesse, Elizabeth, Robert and another daughter.
     7 F   vi   Mary DEVOR, b. Spring Run, Franklin Co., PA.
     8 F   vii Elizabeth DEVOR
     9 F   viii Nancy DEVOR

Joseph DEVOR was a cooper (barrel maker) by trade and was first taxed in Chester County. County records of 1781 show that he was taxed for 100 acres, 2 horses, 3 cows, and four sheep. After the death of his wife, about 1790, he moved to the neighborhood of Chambersburg, then known as Lack Twp., now within the bounds of Franklin Co. His eldest son was already living there and his wife also had died. He and his son married sisters. Joseph's second wife was Sarah Ellen ROLES-RAGAN. Their only child was Albina.

On October 21, 1795, Joseph purchased 129 acres in Path Valley 23 miles from Chambersburg for 1690 pounds sterling which would probably amount to about $200. The land was all woodland and about one mile west of the present village of Spring Run. He built log buildings, cleared the land for cultivation and lived there until his death. Besides clearing the ground for cultivation,

3

stones had to be carried off, which were used to build fences around the fields.

Joseph m. (2) Sarah Ellen ROLES-RAGAN 1790

Children:
    10 F ix   Albina DEVOR. Albina DEVOR married (_____)
               ROBINSON.

Joseph DEVOR was aged and childish when in 1824 he made the following will, recorded in the Franklin Co. Court House. It was written by the Rev. Amos A. McGinley and witnessed by William McCartney.

LAST WILL AND TESTAMENT
In the name of God, Amen, I, Joseph Daver, of Fannett Twp., Franklin Co., Pa being weak in body but of sound mind, do make this my last will and testament vis-
To my wife Sarah, I bequeath 1 cow, 1 hog, 2 sheep, 1 pot, 1 stew kettle. I allow her to take her choice of the cows, sheep, and hogs, also her choice of the pots. I also bequeath to her a bed of her choice, and bedding. Also my dough trough, dresser and its furniture, such as knives and forks, plates, dishes, etc. Also the flour barrel, her clothing and what flax we have now on hand. I likewise bequeath to her during her natural life, the house we now live in and the garden we now occupy, also a sufficiency of firewood to be brought to her by her son Jesse, and what fruit she needs for her own use such as apples, peaches, etc., provided they shall grow on my farm, also four bushels of wheat, four of rye, four of corn, and four of buckwheat, annually during her life. These to be furnished by my son Jesse whom I obligate to keep for her, and her two sheep, and her cow, and to allow her the privilege of raising one hog yearly for her own use.
To my sons James Daver and Jacob Daver I bequeath one dollar each. In favor of my daughter Eleanor, I relinquish all the claims I have against her husband, Joseph Hollingsworth. To my daughters Esther and Albina I bequeath one dollar each in two years after my decease in case they call on them. At the same time also I allow the dollar each to be paid to my sons James and Jacob in case they call on them.
To my son Jesse I bequeath the farm I now reside on, adjoining Robert McCormick and others in Fannett Twp. aforesaid, containing 123 acres, more or less, to be his, his heirs and assigns forever, together with all its appurtenances and all my personal property not specified above. Furthermore, I obligate my son Jesse

to pay all my lawful debts, I also appoint him, Jesse, to be executor of this my will. For the conformation I set my hand and seal to it, and by this act disannul all former wills.

    Signed and sealed this twenty-sixth day of April A.D., one thousand eight hundred and twenty-four.

his

Joseph   X   Daver

mark

    Joseph DEVOR died soon after making this will. His grave is unmarked and unknown, but he must have been buried in the Presbyterian Cemetery at Spring Run, where his son Jesse was later interred.

    The farm passed down through three succeeding generations, until 1910. (Corwin)

SECOND GENERATION

2   James DEVOR, b. ca 1765, Scotland; d. 1842, Spring Run, Franklin Co., PA; bur. Union Cemetery, Amberson Valley, Franklin Co., Pa. (Corwin)

James DEVOR m. (1) Mary Ann Elizabeth TAYLOR.
James DEVOR m. (2) Lydia ROLES, dau. of John ROLES.

    James DEVOR was a Cooper and a member of the U.B. Church and lived at Spring Run, PA. James changed the family name to DEVOR. (Deavor)

Children:
```
+   11 F i     Hannah DEVOR.
+   12 M ii    Joseph DEVOR.
+   13 F iii   Jemima DEVOR.
+   14 M iv    John DEVOR.
+   15 M v     Rolland DEVOR.
+   16 M vi    James DEVOR, Jr.
+   17 M vii   Richard M/E DEVOR.
    18 F viii  Ann DEVOR, b. Spring Run, Franklin Co.
               PA.  She m. (1) Robert GRAHAM.

+   19 F ix    Lydia DEVOR
    20 F x     Catherine DEVOR, b. ca 1812
               Catherine m. (1) Joseph EVITTS.

    21 M xi    Rev. Joshua DEVOR, b. Spring Run, Franklin
               Co., PA.  m. Rachel CLARK, d. in Civil War.
               Joshua was a United Brethren Preacher from
               Bedford Co., PA.
```

3 Jesse DAVER, b. 1771, Chester Co., PA, d. 25 Feb 1833, Spring Run, Franklin Co., PA; bur. Spring Run, Franklin Co., PA.

    Jesse was a farmer in Path Valley. He stayed with his father and cared for him until his death.

Jesse DAVER m. (1) Ruemma "Amy" PETERSON, 1815, Spring Run, Franklin Co., PA. Ruemma, dau. of Robert PETERSON, d. 26 Apr 1858; bur. Spring Run, Franklin Co., PA.
Her brothers were Robert, James and David PETERSON.

Children:
+   22 F i   Jane DEVOR.
+   23 F ii   Mary DEVOR.
+   24 M iii   Joseph DEVOR.
+   25 M iv   James H. DEVOR.
+   26 M v   David H. DEVOR.
+   27 M vi   Jacob J. DEVOR.
   28 F vii   Elizabeth DEVOR, b. 10 Sep 1829, Spring Run, Franklin Co., Pa: d. 17 Dec 1876, Neelyton, Huntingdon Co., Pa; bur. Spring Run. Lived at Neelyton, Huntingdon Co., PA.

                 Elizabeth m. (1) William GILL. William farmed.
                 Children:
                 Amos and Emma GILL.

+   29 M viii Amos McGinley DEVOR.

After his father died Jesse then married, at age 44, and he and his wife cleared more land and built more buildings. On 12 June 1823 Jesse made a Will that bequeathed one third of his property to his wife and the remainder to be divided among his children when they came of age. This Will was written by Rev. Amos McGinley and witnessed by John Ball and Robert Peterson. Jesse signed his Will with Jesse Daver and his tombstone bears the name Deavor. At his death Jesse left eight children ranging in age from eight months to 17 years for his wife to care for. His children changed the family name to DEVOR. (Deavor)
    From a letter by Carrie DEVOR HAWLEY to Mary TAKACH DEVOR, dated 13 Feb 1955: "I knew the Neils that owned the farm between where Ludwigs own and the Mountain were related to us but didn't know how. I see Mrs. Esther NEIL was a sister of Jesse DEVOR. I have heard my dad say that Jesse DEVOR was an Old Devil. He stepped off so many steps of the Neil Place and took it and it was always known as the stripe. We always called it that. I don't know if Ludwigs did.

But I don't get how he could take the land and get clear title to it."

4   Jacob DEAVOR, b. 1779, Chester, PA; d. 3 Apr 1840, Fulton Co., PA; bur. Winegardners Cemetery, Taylor Twp., Fulton Co., PA.
       Jacob was raised a Quaker Presbyterian and died a Methodist. He was an outstanding school teacher. (Deavor)

       Jacob m. (1) Hannah (Pyles) PILES, 31 Oct 1799. Hannah d. 8 Oct 1836, Fulton Co., bur 10 Oct 1836, Winegardners Cemetery, Taylor Twp., Fulton Co., PA.

Children:
+ 30 F i   Martha DEAVOR.
   31 M ii   Philip Piles DEAVOR, b. Taylor Twp., Fulton Co., PA; d. Cassville, PA; bur. Mt. Pleasant, PA. He died unmarried aged twenty-two.

   32 M iii   Joseph Deavor, b. 1804; d. Jan 1877; bur. Clear Ridge, PA.
       Joseph was a shoemaker and lived in Hunt Co. He and his wife were Methodists and had no children.

       Joseph m. (1) Mary HOUCK. Mary, b. ca 1812; d. 1887, Clear Ridge, PA.

   33 F iv   Mary DEAVOR, b. 22 Oct 1806, Springfield, PA; d. 14 Sep 1877, Mt. Pleasant, PA; bur. Clear Ridge Cemetery.
       Mary remained single and lived with her sister Hannah. She was a devout church goer.

+ 34 M v   James DEAVOR.
+ 35 F vi   Annie DEAVOR.
   36 M vii   Jesse DEAVOR, bur. Mt. Pleasant, PA. Drowned at Cook's Station, aged 3 years.

+ 37 M viii Adam DEAVOR.
+ 38 F ix   Hannah DEAVOR.

5   Esther DEVOR, b. Chester, PA. She m. (1) David NEAL, 9 Feb 1797. They cleared land for a home at the foot of the Tuscarora Mt. west of her father's farm in Pennsylvania.

Children:
   39 M i   Henry NEAL, m. Margaret RHINE.

```
40 M ii    David NEAL.
41 F iii   Nancy NEAL, m. (1) George WANDER.    Three
             children.
42 F iv    Elizabeth NEAL, m. (1) Michail KEN.
43 F v     Mary NEAL, m. Baker (_____).
44 F vi    Ruth NEAL, m. Mr. CLAVER.
45 M vii   William NEAL, m. (1) Catherine MILLER.  Nine
             children.
46 F viii  Amy NEAL, m. (1) William SHEARER.     Eight
             children.
47 F ix    Esther NEAL, m. Jacob MILLER.  Ten children.
```

THE DESCENDANTS OF JOSEPH DEVOR

OF PATH VALLEY, PENNSYLVANIA

CHAPTER II

DESCENDANTS OF JAMES DEVOR, SON OF JOSEPH

Eight of James's children left Descendants.
Five male lines and three female lines
are followed as information is available.

They are: Hannah, Joseph, Jemina, John,
Rolland, James, Richard and Lydia.

DESCENDANTS OF HANNAH DEVOR, DAUGHTER OF JAMES

FIRST GENERATION

1   Hannah DEVOR, b. 2 Apr 1788, Spring Run, Franklin Co.,
    Pa; d. 9 Jun 1848.

    Hannah m. (1) Barnabus FEGAN 1809. Barnabus, b. 3 Aug
    1782; d. 15 Aug 1842.

Children:
+   2 M i   Thomas John FEGAN.
    3 F ii   Hannah FEGAN.
    4 F iii Ellen FEGAN.
    5 M iv   James FEGAN.
    6 M v   John FEGAN.
    7 F vi   Nancy Jane FEGAN.
    8 F vii Mary E. FEGAN.
    9 M viii Joseph Devor FEGAN.
   10 F ix   Maria FEGAN.

SECOND GENERATION

2   Thomas John FEGAN, b. Mar 1819; d. 15 Feb 1887.

    Thomas m. (1) Eliza DUNKLE 13 Feb 1834.   Eliza, b.
    1806; d. 11 Apr 1875.

Children:
   11 F i   Mary Ann FEGAN.
+ 12 M ii   Solomon Dunkle FEGAN.
   13 F iii Elizabeth Hannah FEGAN.
   14 M iv   William Penn FEGAN.
   15 F v   Martha D. FEGAN.
   16 M vi   Thomas John FEGAN Jr.
   17 F vii Nancy Elinor FEGAN.

THIRD GENERATION

12 Solomon Dunkle FEGAN, b. 1836; d. 1908.

    Solomon m. (1) Sarah CULBERSON.   Sarah, b. 24 Aug
    1853; d. 15 Apr 1933

Children:
+ 18 M i   Mac Kintire Thomas FEGAN.
   19 F ii   Eliza Blanch FEGAN.
   20 F iii Anna FEGAN.

FOURTH GENERATION

12 Mac Kintire Thomas FEGAN, b. 28 Mar 1871; d. 13 Jun
   1960.

   Mac m. (1) Susanna M. FLICK 1894. Susanna, b. 13 Jun
   1875; d. 25 Feb 1925.

Children:
   21 F i   Ethel Sarah FEGAN, b. 16 Oct 1894; d. 18 Feb
              1975.

              Ethel m. (1) Albert Ray BOYER 1915. Albert,
              b. 14 Jul 1894; d. 30 Oct 1966.

              Children: Lawrence and Dorothy BOYER.

   22 M ii   Ruben L. FEGAN.
   23 F iii Hazel Florence FEGAN.
   24 M iv   Merl S. FEGAN.
   25 F v   Laura FEGAN.
   26 M vi   Theodore M. FEGAN.
   27 M vii Ulysses FEGAN.
   28 F viii Willema FEGAN.
   29 F ix   Ruth E. FEGAN.
   30 M x   Lawrence W. FEGAN.
   31 F xi   Thelma F. FEGAN.
   32 M xii Albert Day FEGAN.
   33 M xiii Merando G. FEGAN.

- -

DESCENDANTS OF JOSEPH DEVOR, SON OF JAMES

FIRST GENERATION

1 Joseph DEVOR, b. ca 1793, Spring Run, Franklin Co.,
   PA; d 1823.

   Joseph m. (1) Ann MORROW 7 Oct 1813, Middle Spring,
   Cumberland Co., PA

Children:
   2 M i   William DEVOR, b. after 1813, Doylesburg,
             PA; chr. 9 Apr 1817.
   3 F ii   Bathsheba DEVOR, b. after 1813, Doylesburg,
             PA; chr. 11 Apr 1816.
   4 F iii Catherine DEVOR, b. 13 Apr 1820.
 + 5 F iv   Agnes DEVOR.

SECOND GENERATION

5   Agnes DEVOR, b. 9 Apr 1823.

    Agnes m. (1) Fred LONG. Fred and Agnes lived at Doylesburg, PA. (Corwin)

Children:
    6 F   i   Bathsheba LONG m. (1) Hance CAMPBELL.
    7 F   ii   Mary Virginia LONG.

- -

DESCENDANTS OF JEMIMA DEVOR, DAUGHTER OF JAMES

FIRST GENERATION

1   Jemima DEVOR, b. abe 1796, Spring Run, Franklin Co., PA.

    Jemima m. William FRENCH, they lived in a log cabin one mile from Spring Run. Both died at Amberson Valley and are buried there. (Corwin)

Children:
    2 F   i   Nancy FRENCH, b. 1828.
    3 M   ii   Solomon FRENCH, b. 1829.
    4 M   iii Robert FRENCH, b. 1832.
    5 M   iv   William FRENCH, Jr, b. 1836.
    6 M   v   Simon FRENCH, b. 1837.

- -

DESCENDANTS OF JOHN DEVOR, SON OF JAMES

FIRST GENERATION

1   John DEVOR, b. 21 Apr 1796, Spring Run, Franklin Co., PA; d. 18 Jan 1879.
John m. (1) Ann THOMPSON 18 Mar 1817, Franklin Co., PA.

Children:
    2 F   i   Catherine DEVOR, b. 13 Apr 1820, Middle Spring, Franklin Co., PA.

            She m. (1) George BERKS 17 Aug 1843, Middle Spring, Franklin Co., PA.

13

```
+   3 F  ii   Agnes Jane DEVOR.
+   4 M  iii  Jacob Peter DEVOR.
+   5 M  iv   David Herron DEVOR.
+   6 M  v    Thompson White DEVOR.
    7 F  vi   Elizabeth Catherine DEVOR, chr. 9 Apr 1834,
              Middle Spring, Franklin Co., PA.

              Elizabeth m. (1) Elias ROSE.

    John m. (2) Mary BARR.
```

SECOND GENERATION

3 Agnes Jane DEVOR, b. 11 Apr 1821, Middle Springs, Franklin Co., PA; d. 18 Sep 1879, Shade Gap, Franklin Co., PA; bur. Pine Grove Cemetery, Shade Gap, PA.

Agnes m. (1) James PETERSON 6 Nov 1845, Middle Spring, Franklin Co., PA.

```
Children:
    8 F  i    Almira Jane PETERSON, b. 30 Dec 1846.
              Almira m. (1) J. Allen McCLAIN 8 Dec 1870.
              Children:
              Jane, Annie, Alfred and Theodore McCLAIN.

    9 F  ii   Annie Elizabeth PETERSON, b. 24 Aug 1838.
              Annie m. (1) W. M. APPLEBY, MD. Feb 1873.

   10 F  iii  Mary Agnes PETERSON, b. 24 Apr 1850; d. 12
              Sep 1892; bur. Shade Gap, Pa.

   11 M  iv   Theodore Calvin PETERSON, b. 8 Nov 1853.
              Theodore m. (1) Annie E. DAVIS 24 Feb 1881.

   12 M  v    Alfred Shade PETERSON, b. 27 Sep 1854.
              Alfred m. (1) Emma SWAN 16 Sep 1879.

   13 F  vi   Amanda Bell PETERSON, b. 5 Sep 1855.
              Amanda m. (1) Walter CLARK  Aug 1881.
```

4 Jacob Peter DEVOR, b. 15 Jun 1822, Roxbury, Franklin Co., PA; d. before 1900, Montgomery Twp, Ashland Co., OH.

Jacob m. (1) Mary Ann HOSSLER 1 Feb 1849, Grandstone Hill, PA. Mary, b. Apr 1830, PA.

```
Children:
   14 M  i    Charles A. DEVOR, b. about 1850, Ashland
              Co., OH; d. 1860.
```

```
    15 F ii      Alice Ann DEVOR, b. about 1854, Ashland Co.,
                 OH; d. 1860.

    16 M iii     John R. DEVOR.
    17 M iv      Jacob Porter DEVOR, b. about 1859.
    18 M v       Horace L. Devor.
    19 F vi      Mary Agnes DEVOR, b. about 1864; d. 1880.
                 Mary m. (1) Harry DOWNS.
                 Children:  Edgar and Helen DOWNS.

+   20 M vii     William Thompson DEVOR.
+   21 M viii    James Edgar DEVOR.
    22 M ix      Samuel DEVOR.
    23 M x       Harry Harvey DEVOR, b. about 1873; d. 1880.

5   David Herron DEVOR, b. 30 Mar 1824, Middle Spring,
    Franklin Co., PA; d. 12 Jan 1890, Cowden, Shelby Co.,
    IL.   In the Civil War he was 1st Sgt. Co. C. 345th
    Illinois Infantry.   He was a Free Methodist preacher
    and a Salvation Army worker.  (Deavor)

    David m. (1) Nancy SICKLES 4 Jul 1850, Hancock Co.,
    OH.  Nancy, dau. of Benjamin SICKLES and Hannah BROWN,
    b. 28 May 1832, Ashtabula, OH; d. 1 Apr 1913, Cowden,
    Shelby Co., IL.

Children:
    24 M i       John T. DEVOR, b. about 1854.
                 John m. (1) Sarah BLACK.

+   25 M ii      Elias DEVOR.
    26 F iii     Sarah Elizabeth DEVOR, b. 18 Aug 1859; d. 8
                 Mar 1932.  She m. (1) Milo THOMAS.  Milo d.
                 12 Dec 1930.

    27 M iv      David Sherman DEVOR, b. 18 Aug 1865.  He m.
                 (1) Nettie TAYLOR.

    28 F v       Hannah Ellen DEVOR, b. 14 Jan 1868, Cowden,
                 Shelby Co., IL; d. 7 Jun 1946, Cowden,
                 Shelby Co., IL; bur. Cowden, IL.

                 Hannah m. (1) Daniel Ezra COCHRAN 7 Oct
                 1884, Cowden, Shelby Co.  Daniel, b. 28 Nov
                 1860, Cowden, Shelby Co., IL; d. 6 Mar 1923,
                 Cowden, Shelby Co., IL; bur. Mound Cemetery,
                 Cowden, IL.
                 Children born at Cowden:
                 Levi, Wallace, Minnie, John, Virgil and
                 Rosena COCHRAN.

+   29 M vi      Jacob A. DEVOR.
```

```
     30 F vii   Nancy May DEVOR, b. 30 Apr 1875; d. 12 Aug
                1926.  Nancy m. (1) C. R. TOLLIVER.


6   Thompson White DEVOR, b. Middle Spring, Franklin Co.,
    PA; chr. 10 Apr 1828, Middle Spring, Franklin Co., PA.
    He joined the Union Army from Ohio and fell in battle.

    Thompson m. (1) Rachel KECKLER.   Rachel b. ca 1832.

Children;
     31 F i     Melinda Jane DEVOR, b. ca 1854.
                Melinda m. (1) David NAFTSGAR.

     32 F ii    Lucille Zella DEVOR, b. ca 1857.
                Lucille m. L. B. FOX.
                Children:  Stella and Earl FOX.

+    33 M iii   Joshua Lafayette DEVOR.
     34 M iv    John C. DEVOR, b. Mar 1861, OH.
                John m. (1) Daisy (_____).



                    THIRD GENERATION

20  William Thompson DEVOR, b. Nov 1866,  m. (1) Minnie
    (_____) Nov 1866.

Children:
     35 M i     Eugene B. DEVOR, b. Apr 1896.
     36 M ii    Marshall B. DEVOR, b. Oct 1897.
     37 F iii   Elinor DEVOR, b. Jul 1899.

21  James Edgar DEVOR, b. ca 1869,  m. (1) Mary ESHELMAN.

Children:
     38 M i     Paul Edgar DEVOR.

25  Elias DEVOR, b. 12 Oct 1856; d. 18 Jul 1933.
    Elias m. Mary (_____).  Mary, b. 1858, IL.

Children:
     39 F i     Tersey E. DEVOR, b. 1891.
     40 M ii    Roland H. DEVOR, b. Sep 1883.
     41 F iii   Goldy O. DEVOR, b. May 1885.
     42 F iv    Stella E. DEVOR, b. Mar 1888.
     43 M v     Frank E. DEVOR, b. Apr 1890.
     44 M vi    Forest A. DEVOR, b Jan 1893.
     45 F vii   Nancy E. DEVOR, b. Dec 1897.
```

29 Jacob A. DEVOR, b. 9 Oct 1870, IL; d. 23 Jul 1941,
Montgomery Co., IL; bur. Mound Cemetery, Shelby Co.,
IL.

Jacob m. (1) Lydia HAZENFELT. Lydia, d. after 1896,
Shelby Co., IL; bur. Mound Cemetery, IL.

Children:
    46 M i   Elmer W. DEVOR, b. Feb 1893.
    47 M ii   David A. DEVOR, b. Feb 1893.
    48 F iii   Eva DEVOR, b. Nov 1895.
    49 F iv   Fay DEVOR, b. May 1896.

Jacob m. (2) Edna (_____). Edna, b. Feb 1871, IL.

Children:
    50 F v   Phoebe J. DEVOR, b. Mar 1899, Francher,
                Shelby Co., IL.

33 Joshua Lafayette DEVOR, b. Jul 1859, IN.

Joshua m. (1) Linnette ROWLAND 22 May 1879, Ashland
Co., OH. Linnette b. 30 Jan 1860, Ashland Co., OH.

Children:
    51 M i   Straub M. DEVOR, b. Mar 1882.
    52 F ii   Gertie B. DEVOR, b. Apr 1884.
    53 M iii   Clyde M. DEVOR, b. Dec 1885.
    54 M iv   William T.A. DEVOR, b. Dec 1887.
    55 F v   Verda B. DEVOR, b. Sep 1891.
    56 F vi   Ruth E. DEVOR, b. Nov 1893.

DESCENDANTS OF ROLLAND DEVOR, SON OF JAMES

1 Rolland DEVOR, b. 1800, Spring Run, Franklin Co., Pa;
   d. 1876, LaGrange, IN. He was a teacher. Went to
   Piqua, OH. As a teacher in those days he ranked among
   the best. His penmanship was superior. He worked for
   John Johnston in Piqua and then went to Elkhart,
   Indiana, where he farmed 100 acres. He was a
   Presbyterian, an abstainer from liquor and tobacco and
   honest in all transactions. (Deavor)

   Rolland m. (1) Elizabeth M. DEFREES in 1824.
   Elizabeth d. 1864.

Children:
   2 F   i   Emma Rebecca DEVOR, b. 1826, Greenville,
               Darke Co., OH; d. 1877, Walkerton, La Porte
               Co., IN.

               Emma m. (1) John COTTON 1845.
               Son Willis COTTON and four other children
               died.

+ 3 M   ii   Joseph Defrees DEVOR.
   4 F   iii   Mary Annette DEVOR, b. 1831, Troy, Miami
               Co., OH.
               Mary m. (1) John H. RERICK, M.D. 1 May
               1856, Elkhart, Elkhart Co., IN.
                  Dr. RERICK was a surgeon in the civil
               War. He served two terms as clerk of
               Lagrange Co., IN. He was editor and
               proprietor of the "Lagrange Standard".
               Children:
               Rolland, John, and Carl RERICK.

   5 M   iv   James Rolland DEVOR, b. abe 1834, Troy,
               Miami Co., OH. James was the inventor of
               several machines. He served in the Civil
               War as Asst. Surgeon and Post Commander.

               James m. (1) Matilda McKIBBEN 15 May 1874,
               Elkhart, Elkhart Co., IN. Matilda d. 1888,
               Goshen, Elkhart Co., IN.

+ 6 M   v   John D. DEVOR.
   7 F   vi   Elizabeth Lavina DEVOR, b. abe 1839,
               Elkhart, Elkhart Co., IN; d 1892, Geneva,
               KS.
               Elizabeth m. (1) Dwight S. LEAVITT 2 Feb
               1864, Elkhart Co., IN.
               Children: Carrie, Newman, and Arthur
               LEAVITT.

8 F vii   Victoria V. DEVOR, b. about 1843, Elkhart,
          Elkhart Co., IN.

          Victoria m. (1) L. L. MERRIFIELD in 1875.
          Children: Hubert MERRIFIELD.

                    SECOND GENERATION

3 Joseph Defrees DEVOR, b. Aug 1828, Piqua, Miami Co.,
   OH. "Joseph had a large experience in drug and
   mercantile business. He has been a bookkeeper at the
   First National Bank of Elkhart, IN for twenty-five
   years. He owns a comfortable home and real estate in
   Elkhart. He is an amateur in music and astronomy and
   continues to study at age 66. He helped much with my
   book." (Deavor 1894)

   Joseph   m. (1) Martha H. STARR in 1851.   Martha d.
   1886.

Children:
   9 F i   Emma Orio DEVOR, b. 1852, Goshen, Elkhart
             Co., IN.
             Emma m. (1) Charles BIBBINS 10 May 1870,
             Elkhart Co., IN.
             Charles was a railway conductor who had been
             a Union soldier and a victim of Libby
             prison. After serving with the railroad, he
             entered the mercantile life in Omaha, NE.
             (Deavor)

  10 M ii   Milton V. DEVOR, b. Feb 1854, Goshen,
             Elkhart Co., IN. Milton was a Printer. He
             and his wife were Methodists.

             Milton m. (1) Frances MERRIFIELD in 1878.

  11 F iii Flora Ellen DEVOR, b. 1856, Syracuse, IN.
             "Flora Ellen is a member of the Presbyterian
             Church and lives at home. She is skilled at
             the art of needlework." (Deavor)

+ 12 M iv   Frank Starr DEVOR.
  13 F v   Marianette DEVOR, b. 1864, Elkhart, Elkhart
             Co., IN.

             Marianette m. (1) Thomas PRITCHARD 1 Jan
             1884, Elkhart, IN.

                         <u>19</u>

Children: Edith and Mildred PRITCHARD.

14 F vi   Victoria DEVOR, b. 1867, Elkhart, Elkhart
           Co., IN. "Victoria is a Presbyterian and a
           stenographer and typewriter of marked
           ability." (Deavor 1896)

6 John D. DEVOR, b. May 1836, Troy, Miami Co., OH.

John m. (1) Fannie MATTINGLY in 1862. Fannie died six
months after the marriage.

John m. (2) Cornelia M. LUSK, Dayton, Montgomery Co.,
OH. Cornelia, b. Oct 1836, MA.

Children:
15 M i   William R. DEVOR, b. Aug 1864. William is
           a printer and lives in WI. He m. (1) Clara
           J. (_____). Clara b. Feb 1866, WI.

16 F ii   Cornelia DEVOR.
17 F iii   Fannie DEVOR.
18 M iv   John DEVOR. John practiced law for several
           years and entered Journalism, establishing
           papers in Goshen, Plymouth, Lagrange and
           Elkhart, IN and in Wauseon OH, Galesburg IL
           and Elkham WI. He then became a banker and
           a dealer in commercial paper.

           John m. Cornelia (_____). He lived with her
           at Reedsburg, WI. His daughter Cornelia is
           married and also lives in WI. (Deavor)

THIRD GENERATION

12 Frank Starr DEVOR m. (1) Sadie A. BOYER   Aug 1887.
   Sadie, b. Oct 1866, Elkhart Co., IN.

Children:
   19 F i   Orie M. DEVOR, b. Oct 1889.
   20 F ii   Ethelyn DEVOR, b. Apr 1892.

DESCENDANTS OF JAMES DEVOR, SON OF JAMES

1   James DEVOR, b. 11 Nov 1801, Spring Run, Franklin
    Co., PA; d. 7 May 1881, Three Springs, Huntingdon Co.,
    PA; bur. Three Springs, Huntingdon Co., PA.

    James m. (1) Rebecca FLOCK (FLECK). Rebecca, b. 8 Dec
    1801; d. 16 Aug 1870, Three Springs, PA; bur. Three
    Springs, PA.

    James was a contracting mason. He lived at Three
    Springs, Huntingdon Co., PA. Houses he built were in
    use and well preserved in 1896. He was a Methodist.
    (Deavor)

Children:
+ 2 M   i   J. Edward DEVOR.
+ 3 M   ii   Basil J. DEVOR.
   4 F   iii   Elizabeth DEVOR. Lived in Cromell Twp.,
               Huntingdon Co., PA.
               Elizabeth m. (1) Jacob G. SWOPE.

   5 F   iv   Mary Ann DEVOR. Lived in Saltillo, PA.
               Mary m. (1) Harrison WAGNER.

   6 F   v   Hannah DEVOR lived in Allegheny Co, PA.
               Hannah m. (1) George S. MILLER.

   7 F   vi   Margaret "Maggie" DEVOR.
               Margaret m. (1) Samuel WILLET.

   8 F   vii   Jennie DEVOR, bur. Three Springs, PA,
               unmarried.

SECOND GENERATION

2   J. Edward DEVOR, b. Nov 1827. J. Edward was educated
    in the public schools, Mittenwood Academy and Mt.
    Pleasant College. He taught at Harrisburg, PA. He
    was a member of the 5th St. M.E. Church.

    Edward m. (1) Lizzie SHOPE. (Deavor)

Children:
   9 M   i   Harry C. DEVOR, b. Harrisburg, Dauphin Co.,
               PA.

3   Basil J. DEVOR, b. 29 Oct 1829, Franklin Co., PA; d.
    9 Nov 1905. Basil lived at Mt. Union, PA. He
    attended public schools, Mittenwood Academy and Mt.
    Pleasant College. He was a surveyor, teacher, a Civil

War engineer and a member of the Flint Glass Sand Co. He was admitted to the Hunt County Bar in 1878.

Basil m. (1) Margaret FAUST, Margaret, b. Jun 1833, PA.

Children:
+ 10 M i Gerald L. DEVOR.
  11 F ii Emma Lease DEVOR.
  12 F iii Lizzie Ida DEVOR.

THIRD GENERATION

10 Gerald L. DEVOR, b. Jul 1858, IN.

Gerald m. (1) Nellie COLEMAN. Nellie, b. Jun 1861.

Children:
  13 M i Ray DEVOR, b. Oct 1884, Chicago, Cook Co., IL.
  14 M ii Earl DEVOR, b. Aug 1889.

- -

DESCENDANTS OF RICHARD M/E DEVOR, SON OF JAMES

FIRST GENERATION

1 Richard M/E DEVOR, b. about 1803, Spring Run, Franklin Co., PA; d. about 1870, Cumberland Co., PA; bur. Cumberland Co., PA.

Richard M/E m. (1) Leah SHREINER 29 Jul 1829, Newville, Cumberland Co., PA. Leah, dau. of Elias SHREINER, b. 20 Dec 1804, PA; d. 21 Mar 1869, Cumberland Co., PA; bur. Newburg, Cumberland Co., PA.

Children:
+ 2 M i Richard M. DEVOR.
  3 M ii Lemuel DEVOR, b. about 1837.
  4 F iii Nancy DEVOR, b. about 1838.
  5 F iv Caroline DEVOR, b. about 1840.
  6 F v Catherine M.D. DEVOR, b. 1842; d. Mar 1844.
  7 M vi Elias DEVOR, b. about 1846.
  8 F vii Margaret DEVOR, b. about 1848.

SECOND GENERATION

2   Richard M. DEVOR, b. 23 Nov 1831/1833; d. 12 Jan 1912.
Carlisle, Cumberland Co., PA; bur. Carlisle,
Cumberland Co., PA.

Richard m. (1) Nancy Ann GRAHAM 1 Jul 1854 Cumberland
Co., PA. Nancy, dau of John GRAHAM and Lydia DEVOR,
(dau of James Devor, see same), b. 5 Jul 1831,
Cumberland Co., PA; d. 18 Mar 1885, Cumberland Co.,
PA.

Children:
+   9 M   i   William J. DEVOR.
   10 M   ii   David S. DEVOR, b. 15 Jul 1857; d. 1 Jul
               1927; bur. Kirkwood, Warren Co., IL.
               David m. (1) Laura BELL.

   11 M   iii John DEVOR, b. 1860.
   12 M   iv   Gates Ellmore Ellsworth DEVOR.
   13 F   v   Mary DEVOR, b 1866.
   14 F   vi   Leah DEVOR, b. 1868.
   15 M   vii Joseph DEVOR, b. 1871, Polk Co., IA.
               Joseph m. (1) Alma CARBAUGH.
   16 M   viii Albert DEVOR, b. 1873; d. 1916.
   17 M   ix   Bradford DEVOR, b. 1875; d. Bakersfield,
               Kern Co., CA.

Richard M. DEVOR m. (2) Emma C. FOUST 6 Oct 1892,
Carlisle, Cumberland Co., PA. Emma, b. about 1857; d.
Jan 1926, Shippensburg, Cumberland Co., PA.

Children:
   18 F   x   Edith Jane DEVOR, b. 24 Feb 1892, Carlisle,
               Cumberland Co., PA.
   19 F   xi   Catherine Naomi DEVOR, b. 24 Mar 1896,
               Carlisle, Cumberland Co., PA.

THIRD GENERATION

9   William J. DEVOR, b. Feb 1856. Res: Southampton
Twp., Cumberland Co., PA, 1900.

William m. (1) Susanna A. (_____). Susanna, b. Jan
1871, PA.

Children:
   20 M   i   Ambrose DEVOR, b. May 1889, Cumberland Co.,
               PA.
   21 F   ii   Ardella DEVOR, b. Jul 1891, Cumberland Co.,
               PA.

23

```
22 F iii   Mary DEVOR, b.   Mar 1894, Cumberland Co.,
           PA.
23 M iv    Earl Raphel DEVOR, b.   Apr 1896, Cumberland
           Co., PA.
24 M v     William DEVOR, b.   Aug 1898.
```

16 Gates Ellmore Ellsworth DEVOR, b. 7 Oct 1861, Newburg,
Cumberland Co., PA; d. 31 Dec 1924, Ponemah, Warren
Co., IL; bur. Center Grove Cemetery, Warren Co., IL.

Gates m. (1) Susan CARBAUGH 5 Oct 1888, Walnut Bottom,
Cumberland Co., PA. Susan, dau. of Augustus CARBAUGH
and Catherine M. HARDY, b. 23 Oct 1862, Franklin,
Adams Co., PA; d. 11 Nov 1951, Keosauqua, Van Buren
Co., IA; bur. Center Grove Cemetery, Kirkwood, IL.

```
Children:
   25 M i     Richard Augustus "Lloyd" DEVOR, b. 8 Apr
             1889, Jacksonville, Cumberland Co., Pa; d.
             Oct 1957, Middleton, IA; bur. Center Grove
             Cemetery, Warren Co., IL.

             Richard m. (1) Isabel SOUTHWICK 19 May 1917.

+  26 F ii    Katherine Laura "Belle" DEVOR.
   27 F iii   Frances Ella Mae DEVOR, b. 15 Oct 1892,
             Kirkwood, Warren Co., IL; d. 24 Mar 1968;
             bur. Monmouth, Warren Co., IL.

             Frances m. (1) Robert Wesley JONES 24 Jun
             1916.

   28 F iv    Mary Elizabeth DEVOR, b. 11 Apr 1894,
             Kirkwood, Warren Co., IL; d. 17 Jul 1937,
             Bentonsport, Van Buren Co., IA.

             Mary m. (1) Ed G. JONES 20 Jan 1915.

+  29 M v     Joseph Mansfield DEVOR.
```

FOURTH GENERATION

26 Katherine Laura "Belle" DEVOR, b. 19 Oct 1890,
Jacksonville, Cumberland Co., PA; d. 28 May 1953,
Keosauqua, Van Buren Co., IA; bur. Bonaparte, Van
Buren Co., IA.

Katherine m. (1) Melvin Ernest MORRIS 17 Jan 1923,
Stronghurst, Warren Co., IL. Melvin, son of Stephen

Riley MORRIS and Sarah A. HILLIARD, b. 5 Aug 1894, Granger, Scotland Co., MO; d. 21 Aug 1978, Keosauqua, Van Buren Co., IA; bur. Bonaparte, IA.

Children:
30 M i   Donald Eugene MORRIS, b. 17 Dec 1923, Granger, Scotland Co., MO; d. 24 Jan 1982, Iowa City, Johnson Co., IA.

Donald m. (1) Helen HACKARD 18 Sep 1948, Keosauqua, Van Buren Co., IA. Helen, dau. of Fred HACKARD and Fay HEMINGER, b. 28 Feb 1923; d. 11 Aug 1977; bur. Mount Sterling, IA.

31 M ii   Roland "Darrell" MORRIS, b. 22 Apr 1925, Mount Sterling, Van Buren Co., IA.

Roland m. (1) Marie CHAPPIS 10 Apr 1948, Fairfield, Jefferson Co., IA. Marie, b. 26 Sep 1926, Salena, Jefferson Co., IA.

32 F iii   Avis Darlene MORRIS, b. 11 Feb 1927, Mount Sterling, Van Buren Co., IA.

Avis m. (1) Vincent Henry BOHNENKAMP 12 Jan 1948, Fort Madison, Lee Co., IA. Vincent, son of Henry A. BOHNENKAMP and Catherine Ann STRUNK, b. 21 Aug 1923, West Point, Lee Co., IA.

33 M iv   Leslie Edward MORRIS, b. 14 Oct 1928, Mount Sterling, Van Buren Co., IA; d. 15 Jan 1972, Van Buren Co., IA; bur. Bonaparte, Van Buren Co., IA.

Leslie m. (1) Mary Louise NEAL 4 Jun 1962, Keosaqua, Van Buren Co., IA.

29 Joseph Mansfield DEVOR, b. 2 May 1896, Kirkwood, Warren Co., IL; d. Pontiac, Oakland Co., MI.

Joseph m. (1) Lottie CAMPER 14 Jun 1915.

Children:
34 F i   Dorothy DEVOR, b. about 1921, IL.

Dorothy m. (1) Reid GRAHAM about 1950.

Children: Daniel Reid GRAHAM.

35 F ii   Doris DEVOR, b. about 1923, IL.

DESCENDANTS OF LYDIA DEVOR, DAUGHTER OF JAMES

FIRST GENERATION

1 Lydia DEVOR, b. about 1812, Franklin Co., PA; d. 1860/1870, Cumberland Co., PA.

Lydia m. (1) John GRAHAM.

Children:
```
  2 F   i    Nancy Ann GRAHAM,

            Nancy m. Richard M. DEVOR, descendant of
            Richard M/E DEVOR.  See same.

  3 M   ii   William GRAHAM, b. about 1834.
  4 M   iii  James GRAHAM.
  5 F   iv   Elizabeth GRAHAM, b. about 1838.
  6 F   v    Mary J. GRAHAM, b. about 1840.
  7 F   vi   Catherine GRAHAM, b. 1841.
  8 M   vii  David GRAHAM, b about 1843.
  9 M   viii Roles GRAHAM, b. about 1844.
 10 F   ix   Margaret GRAHAM, b. about 1848.
 11 M   x    John GRAHAM, b. about 1850.
 12 F   xi   Sarah GRAHAM, b. about 1853.
```

THE DESCENDANTS OF JOSEPH DEVOR

OF PATH VALLEY, PENNSYLVANIA

CHAPTER III

DESCENDANTS OF JESSE DAVER/DEAVOR, SON OF JOSEPH

Jesse's children changed their name to DEVOR.
Seven of Jesse's children left descendants.
Five male lines and two female lines
are followed as far as information is available

They are: Jane, Mary, Joseph,
James, David, Jacob and Amos.

DESCENDANTS OF JESSE DAVER/DEAVOR, SON OF JOSEPH

FIRST GENERATION

1 Jane DEVOR, b. 12 Mar 1816, Spring Run, Franklin Co., PA; d. 24 Dec 1893, Spring Run, Franklin Co., PA; bur., Spring Run, Franklin Co., PA.

Jane Devor m. (1) David FRENCH 1841/1842, Spring Run, Franklin Co., PA. David, son of James A. FRENCH.

David was a cooper and farmed in Franklin County.

Children:
+ 2 M   i   Joseph FRENCH.
+ 3 M   ii   William FRENCH.
+ 4 F   iii   Melvina FRENCH.
+ 5 F   iv   Margaret FRENCH.
+ 6 F   v   Amy FRENCH.
   7 F   vi   Lucinda FRENCH m. (1) John SANNO.
   8 F   vii   Mary FRENCH.
   9 F   viii Jemima Jane FRENCH, died at age 20 years. (Corwin)

David and Jane had a small farm near the Devor home in Franklin Co. and raised a family of 8 children. This family all remained in Path Valley. Rev. Mower conducted Jane's funeral in 1893, burial at Spring Run. (Deavor)

SECOND GENERATION

2 Joseph FRENCH, b. 1842; d. 1914; bur., Spring Run, Franklin Co., PA.

Joseph FRENCH m. (1) Maria "Jennie" Jane HAMMOND.

Joseph was a teacher of wide reputation. He entered the Civil War for 9 months and then enlisted for three years. He was in Libby prison. (from hard to read tombstone.) (Corwin)

Children:
+ 10 F i   Elizabeth "Lizzie" FRENCH.
   11 F ii   Miriam Grace FRENCH.
               Miriam m. (1) (_____) NEISWANDER.

3. William FRENCH, b. 12 Jul 1844; d. 15 Oct 1890.
               William served in the Civil War. (Corwin)

William m. (1) Sarah B. CROUSE.

Children:
```
    12 M i    Ulysses G. FRENCH.
    13 F ii   Alice FRENCH.
    14 F iii  Myrtle FRENCH.
    15 M iv   George FRENCH.
    16 F v    Bessie FRENCH.
    17 F vi   Sadie FRENCH.
    18 F vii  Charlotte FRENCH.
```

4   Melvina FRENCH, b. 1846; d. 1902.

Melvina m. (1) James McCLAIN 1881.   He was a Farmer.

Children:
```
    19 F i    Sarah "Sadie" McCLAIN, b. Sep 1881.
```

5   Margaret FRENCH, b. 12 Jan 1848; d. 6 Jul 1901.

Margaret m. (1) Solomon B. CROUSE.   Solomon, son of
George CROUSE and Miss (_____).

Zella Forrester said Margaret was the second wife of
Solomon Crouse.

Children:
```
+   20 M i    William Crouse.
    21 F ii   Bertha "Bertie" CROUSE.
              Bertha lived in Canton, OH with her half
              brother Ed CROUSE after his wife Grace died.
              (Anna)

+   22 F iii  Stella CROUSE.
+   23 M iv   Solomon Warren "Sol" CROUSE.
```

6   Amy FRENCH.   Amy m. (1) William RICHARDSON.

Children:
```
    24 F i    Mabel RICHARDSON.
```

THIRD GENERATION

10 Elizabeth "Lizzie" FRENCH, b. 31 Jan 1867; d. 29 Dec.
    1942; bur., Spring Run Cemetery, Spring Run, Franklin
    Co., PA

    "Lizzie" m. (1) Howard LOVE.   Howard, b. 20 Mar 1863;
    d. 19 Jun 1898; bur., Spring Run Cemetery, Spring Run,
    Franklin Co., PA.

Children:
+   25 F i   Grace Beryl LOVE.
    26 U ii   Infant LOVE.

20 William CROUSE, b. 27 Aug 1821; d. 24 May 1874.

    William Crouse m. (1) Susannah NEIL. Susannah, b. 13
    Sep 1825; d. 1900, Chambersburg, PA.

Children:
+   27 M i   John Dallas CROUSE.

22 Stella CROUSE, b. 1881; d. 1946.
   Stella m. (1) Isaac WILSON.

Children:
    28 F i   Thelma WILSON, b. 20 Nov 1903; d. 23 Jun
                1980.
    29 F ii   Hazel WILSON, b. 29 Jun 1902; d. 4 Dec 1981.
    30 F iii   Kathleen WILSON.
    31 M iv   Norman WILSON.
    32 M v   Warren WILSON, 73 yr, b. 1908; d. 1981
    33 F vi   Faye WILSON.
    34 M vii   James WILSON.
    35 M viii   Wesley WILSON.
    36 M ix   David WILSON.

23 Solomon Warren "Sol" CROUSE, b. 19 Dec 1885, Fannett
   Twp., Franklin Co., Pa; d. 2 Jun 1946, Indiana, PA;
   bur., Braceville Cemetery, Newton Falls, Oh.

   Solomon m. (1) Sarah Ann DEVOR 12 Sep 1912. Sarah,
   dau. of Doras McGinley DEVOR and Alice Ida HAMMOND, b.
   29 May 1887, Spring Run, Fannett Twp, Franklin Co.,
   PA; d. 15 Sep 1953, Warren, Trumbull Co., OH; bur.,
   Braceville Cemetery, Newton Falls, OH.

        Sol and Sarah were cousins. See Sarah at #28
   daughter of Doras Devor #6, son of Jacob (Chap. III).
        At the time of the marriage of Sarah and Sol, he
   was living at Phalanx, OH. He was employed as a
   conductor for the railroad company at Phalanx where
   they made their home. They moved to Warren in 1917
   where he worked in the Store Room Dept. at the
   Republic Steel for 29 years.
        Sol died of a heart attack at the wheel of his
   car in Indiana, PA. when he and Sarah were enroute to
   Shippensburg, PA. to attend the funeral of his sister
   Stella. (Anna)

Children:
    37 U i   (_____) CROUSE. This child was born dead.

FOURTH GENERATION

25 Grace Beryl LOVE, b. 1892; d. Sep 1966, FL.

Grace m. (1) Herbert "Uncle Dudley" "Herb" TICE.

Children:
  38 F i   Margaret "Peg" TICE. (Anna)

  39 F ii   Ruth TICE. (Anna)

27 John Dallas CROUSE, b. 5 Jan 1847, Spring Run, Franklin Co., PA; d. 17 Jan 1920, Willow Hill, Franklin Co., Pa.

John m. (1) Melvina Eliza Narcessa WILSON 27 Jan 1870. Melvina, dau. of Mathew Cowan WILSON, and Margaret BAIR, b. 19 Jan 1852, Knob, Spring Run, Franklin Co., PA; d. 27 May 1946, Willow Hill, PA.

Children:
+ 40 M i   William West CROUSE.

FIFTH GENERATION

40 William West CROUSE, b. 20 Sep 1870, Shadwell, VA; d. 21 Jul 1955, Willow Hill, PA

William m. (1) Hannah Jane "Jennie" BURKE Apr 1890. Hannah, dau. of James BURKE and Mary Ann BRANDT, b. 8 Mar. 1869, Willow Hill, PA; d. 17 Mar 1950, Willow Hill, PA.

Children:
+ 41 F i   Mabel Zelda CROUSE, 46 yr.

SIXTH GENERATION

41 Mabel Zelda CROUSE, b. 6 Mar 1899, Willow Hill, PA; d. July 1945, Harrisburg, PA.

Mabel m. (1) Lyle Wood CAMPBELL, Sep 1919. Lyle, son of William Alexander CAMPBELL, and Cora Nettie SKINNER, b. 18 Nov 1900, Dry Run, PA; d. 4 Apr 1925, Dry Run, PA.

Children;
+ 42 M i   Jack Crouse CAMPBELL.

42 Jack Crouse CAMPBELL, b. 9 Mar 1922

    Jack m. (1) Lavina Mae HAMMOND 27 Nov 1947. Lavina,
    dau of George Washington Shearer HAMMOND and Ruth
    Barclay STITT, b. 23 Oct 1926.
        Lavina was a hairdresser at the Empress Salon in
    Harrisburg, PA and a homemaker.

        "The couple married Nov. 27, 1947, at Upper Path
        Valley Presbyterian Church in Spring Run, PA.
        Before retiring, Jack was a maintenance
        management specialist for the Department of
        Defense, AMCCOM, Rock Island (IL) Arsenal, where
        he was employed 33 years. He served three years
        in the U.S. Navy during World War II. They are
        members of St. Mark's Presbyterian Church of
        Bayonet Point. They are winter residents of New
        Port Richey, FL and were honored at a party on
        the occasion of their 50th Wedding Anniversary."
        (Mrs. Jack Campbell)

Children:
+   43 M i   Dr. Lyle Crouse CAMPBELL.
+   44 F ii   Linda Mae CAMPBELL.

43   Dr. Lyle Crouse CAMPBELL, b. 4 Apr 1950, Spring
    Run, PA.

    Lyle m. (1) Donna ELLIS 3 Sep 1977. Donna, b. 30 Apr
    1952. In 1997 they live at Glenwood, IL.

Children:
    45 M i   Brendan CAMPBELL.
    46 F ii   Cara Elizabeth CAMPBELL, b. 30 Jul 1984,
               Hazelcrest, IL.

44 Linda Mae CAMPBELL, b. 10 Aug 1951.

    Linda m. (1) Paul David MALMGREN 7 Sep 1974. Paul, b.
    14 Mar 1951, Chicago, IL. In 1997 they were living at
    Sister Bay.

Children:
    47 M i   Jeffrey Nels MALMGREN, b. 21 May 1981,
               Joliet, IL. Lived at Sister Bay in 1997.

    48 F ii   April Linnea MALMGREN, b. 10 Mar 1986,
               Chicago, IL; d. 14 Sep 1986, Chicago, IL;

bur. Chicago, IL.   Death was by Sudden Death
Syndrome.   (Lavina)

49 F iii   Karena Noelle MALMGREN, b. 12 Dec 1987,
Chicago, IL.

- -

THE DESCENDANTS OF MARY DEVOR, DAUGHTER OF JESSE

FIRST GENERATION

1   Mary DEVOR, b. 15 Mar 1818, Spring Run, Franklin Co.,
PA;   d. 30 Jun 1906, Spring Run, probably.

Mary m. (1) Henry SHEARER, Spring Run, Franklin Co.,
Pa.   Henry, b. 1816; d. 27 Dec 1851.

Henry SHEARER froze to death on his way home one
night while intoxicated.   He left Mary with 8 small
children and no provisions.   Her brother gave Mary a
small piece of land from the home farm and built her
a log cabin.   The children were put out for their keep
and turned out well.   (Deavor) (DeVore)

Children:
+   2 M   i   Amos SHEARER.
+   3 F   ii   Jane SHEARER.
+   4 M   iii   Jonathan SHEARER.
+   5 M   iv   Jesse SHEARER.
+   6 M   v   William SHEARER.
+   7 M   vi   David SHEARER.
+   8 F   vii   Emma SHEARER.
+   9 M   viii   Michael SHEARER.

Mary DEVOR m. (2) David GAMBLE.
   Both Mary and David were very old when they
married.   In the book "Deavor Family" by Rev. W.T.S.
Deavor his name is spelled Gambell.

SECOND GENERATION

2   Amos SHEARER, b. 12 Aug 1838; d. 18 Jun 1902.

Amos m. (1) Margaret Ann HAMMOND 25 Dec. 1860, (Church
Record, 26 Nov 1860).   Margaret, dau. of Phillip
HAMMOND and Mariah CRAMER, b. 4 Mar 1839; d. 26 May
1904.

Amos served in the Civil War. (Deavor)

Children:
```
    10 F i      Teresa Ida SHEARER, b. 24 Jan 1862; d. 1928;
                bur. Stenger Cemetery, Ft. Louden, PA.

                Teresa m. (1) James SHULTZ 25 Jul 1900, Ft.
                Louden, PA.  James, bur. Stenger Cemetery,
                Ft. Louden, Pa.

    11 F ii     Mary Susan Shearer, b. 5 Apr 1864.
  + 12 M iii    Philip West SHEARER.
  + 13 M iv     David Henry SHEARER.
  + 14 M v      William Harvey SHEARER.
    15 M vi     John Alfred SHEARER, b. 11 Aug 1873; d. 14
                May 1960.

                John m. (1) Eleanor Bernice SHARP 22 Feb
                1902.  Eleanor, b. 12 Oct 1876; d. 27 Feb
                1902.

    16 F vii    Annie or Anna M. SHEARER, b. 22 Jun 1876; d.
                1946.

                Annie m. (1) Carl J. ADAM 25 Aug 1900.
                Carl, b. 1859; d. 1940.

    17 F viii   Martha Ann SHEARER.
    18 M ix     Michael J. SHEARER, b. 1878.
  + 19 F x      Bessie Mae SHEARER.
```

3 Jane SHEARER m. (1) Elisha Kling. He was a cabinet
   maker and lived at Mt. Joy. (Deavor)

Children:
```
    20 M i      Henry KLING m. (1) Ora SWAN.
    21 M ii     Robert KLING.
    22 M iii    Jesse KLING m. (1) Mary KUHN.
    23 M iv     George KLING.
    24 M v      Charles KLING.
    25 F vi     Elizabeth KLING.
    26 F vii    Margaret KLING.
    27 F viii   Jane KLING.
    28 F ix     Martha KLING.
```

4 Jonathan SHEARER m. (1) Ellen CROUSE.

Children:
```
    29 F i      Mary SHEARER m. (1) William CLARKE.
    30 F ii     Hannah SHEARER.
```

5   Jesse SHEARER m. (1) Elizabeth CROUSE.

Children:
    31 F i   Ida SHEARER
    32 F ii   Margaret SHEARER.

6   William SHEARER m. (1) Laura FINK.

Children:
    33 M i   Lyman SHEARER.
    34 F ii   Clara SHEARER.

7   David SHEARER m. Jane CLARKE.

Children:
    35 M i   John SHEARER.
    36 F ii   Maude SHEARER.
    37 F iii   Mary SHEARER.
    38 F iv   Ellen SHEARER.

8   Emma SHEARER m. (1) John P. NESBITT.

Children:
    39 M i   John NESBITT.
    40 F ii   Mary NESBITT.
    41 M iii   William NESBITT.
    42 M iv   Shearer NESBITT.
    43 M v   Jesse NESBITT.
    44 M vi   Amos NESBITT.
    45 F vii   Etna NESBITT.
    46 M viii Jones NESBITT.
    47 M ix   Thomas NESBITT.

9   Michael SHEARER m. (1) Jane CAMPBELL.
        A picture in a Path Valley Newspaper of Aug 1982
        shows Michael and Jane Shearer at the 1916 Path
        Valley Picnic with seventeen of their
        descendants. The picnics were started in 1907.

Children:
    48 F i   Mary SHEARER.
    49 F ii   Grace SHEARER.
    50 M iii   Jesse SHEARER.
    51 M iv   Clark SHEARER.
    52 F v   Jennie SHEARER.
    53 M vi   Frank SHEARER.
    54 M vii   Paul SHEARER.
    55 F viii Ruth SHEARER.
    56 F ix   Margaret SHEARER.

THIRD GENERATION

12 Philip West SHEARER, b. 20 Sep 1866; d. 10 Jan 1921;
bur. Paradise Cemetery.

Philip m. (1) Mary Elizabeth McCLAIN 4 Jul 1888,
Fannettsburg, PA. Mary, b. 16 Oct 1866; d. 6 Nov
1946.
      They lived at Fannettsburg and Lancaster, PA.
Philip West SHEARER died of cancer.

Children:
    57 F i   Ethel May SHEARER, b. 17 Dec 1888; d. 18 Apr
                1945.

                Ethel m. (1) Ralph A. KURTZ.
                Children:
                Mary, Raymond and Greta KURTZ.

    58 F ii   Edna SHEARER, b. 19 Dec 1889.

                Edna m. (1) Watson E. FRYMYER. Watson, b.
                28 Jun 1889.

    59 F iii   Ruth Margaret SHEARER, b. 3 Mar 1893.

                Ruth m. John Kuezer HURST.
                Children: Evelyn HURST.

 + 60 M iv   Raymond Dwight SHEARER.
    61 M v   Karl or Earl Alexander SHEARER, b. 5 Oct
                1896; d. 1 Dec 1896.

 + 62 M vi   Monte Clair SHEARER.
    63 F vii   Helen Elizabeth SHEARER, b. 7 Oct 1879.

                Helen m. (1) Harry E. CABLE.
                Children:
                Jean, Richard, Nelda and Donald CABLE.

 + 64 M viii Frederick Clair McClain SHEARER.
    65 M ix   John S. SHEARER, b. 27 Dec 1902; d. 19 Mar
                of diphtheria; bur. Paradise Cemetery.

    66 M x   Herbert West SHEARER, b. 16 Jul 1904; d. 3
                Feb 1907.

    67 F xi   Mary Kathryn SHEARER, b. 20 Feb 1907,
                Paradise.

                Mary m. Ralph ULRICH 21 Sep 1927.
                Children: Nancy and John ULRICH.

68 F xii   Emma   Mildred   SHEARER,   m.   (1)   John   L.
            CARPENTER.

13 David Henry SHEARER, b. 26 Mar 1869; d. 11 Mar 1950;
bur. Path Valley Cemetery, PA.

    David m. Catherine Blanch DOYLE 18 Feb 1892.
Catherine, b. 8 Feb 1870; d. 26 Feb 1952; bur. Path
Valley Cemetery, PA.

        Mr. & Mrs. SHEARER had a 50th Wedding Anniversary
18 Feb 1942.

Children:
    69 F i   Anna Creigh SHEARER, b. 13 Jul 1892.

                Anna m. (1) William J. GURY 22 Oct 1912.
                William, b. 7 Aug 1881; d. 17 Jul 1950.
                Children: Francis, Jay and Anna GURY.

    70 F ii   Lola Vernal SHEARER, b. 14 Oct 1893; d. 2
                Oct 1894.

+   71 M iii   Lyman Bruce SHEARER.
+   72 M iv   Frederick Carl SHEARER.
    73 M v   Amos Harold SHEARER, b. 11 May 1902; d. 3
                Sep 1902.

    74 F vi   Dorothy Mae SHEARER, b. 22 Aug 1903; d. 26
                Jan 1919 in flu epidemic.

    75 M vii   William West SHEARER, b. 22 Feb 1906; d. 18
                Jan 1919 in flu epidemic.

    76 M viii   Bert Doyle SHEARER, b. 27 Mar 1909; d. 24
                Jan 1955.

                Bert m. (1) Irene GROCE 26 Jun 1932. Irene,
                b. 16 Apr 1912.

    77 M ix   Infant son SHEARER, b. 2 Oct 1913; d. 2 Oct
                1913.

14 William Harvey SHEARER, b. 2 Jan 1871; d. 26 Feb 1952.
William was a mail carrier.

    William m. (1) Anna Sarah BAKER 24 Oct 1894, by Rev.
Dobbin. Anna, b. 29 Jun 1868; d. 25 Jan 1932.

```
Children:
    78 F   i    Lillian SHEARER, b. 13 Mar 1895.
    79 F   ii   Alma Hope SHEARER, b. 24 Jan 1897.

                Alma m. (1) Gill CLIPPINGER 13 Dec 1919, Ft.
                Louden, PA.  Gill d. 14 Jul 1971; bur. St.
                Thomas, PA.
                Children:  Gill CLIPPINGER.

+   80 M   iii  Leroy SHEARER.
+   81 M   iv   Harvey Donald SHEARER.
+   82 M   v    Earl James SHEARER.
    83 M   vi   Romain Carl SHEARER, b. 9 Mar 1905; d. 25
                Mar 1928.
                    Romain was electrocuted while working
                on the electric lines at Saxton, PA.

    84 F   vii  Elizabeth May SHEARER, b. 24 Jun 1907.

                Elizabeth  m.  (1)  Paul  BUTTS  Oct  1927,
                Hagerstown, PA by Rev. Claver.
                Paul, b. 5 Jun 1905; d. 19 Apr 1961; bur.,
                St. Thomas.
                Children:  Paul Butts.

    85 F   viii Ida Margarita SHEARER, b. 12 Mar 1910.

                Ida m. (1) Charles Alfred FRIES 19 Dec 1936,
                Hagerstown, MD.  Charles, b. 27 Feb 1912; d.
                21 Dec 1953.
                    Alfred and Ida had no children.  After
                Charles died Ida lived with her sister
                Elizabeth May SHEARER BUTTS on Route 4,
                Chambersburg, PA.

19 Bessie Mae SHEARER, b. 9 Oct 1880; d. 31 Jul 1970.

    Bessie m. (1) Jack PLUEBELL 24 Sep 1901, Pittsburg,
    PA.  Jack, b. 19 Aug 1878; d. 7 Apr 1947.
        Mrs.   Jack   Pluebell,   114  McMaster   Drive,
    Monroeville, PA. was 88 years old in 1969.  She spent
    Christmas in bed and every day after until she died.

Children:
    86 M   i    Kenneth PLUEBELL
    87 F   ii   Velma PLUEBELL
    88 M   iii  John PLUEBELL.   He built a house in Metal
                Twp., PA.

    89 M   iv   William PLUEBELL.
    90 F   v    Bessie PLUEBELL m. Frank BONNIE or BONNER.
    91 U   vi   Given PLUEBELL.
```

```
92 M vii   David PLUEBELL.
93 M viii  Edwin PLUEBELL.
94 M ix    Raymond PLUEBELL.
95 M x     Robert PLUEBELL.
```

FOURTH GENERATION

60 Raymond Dwight SHEARER, b. 3 Oct 1895,
       Fannettsburg, PA; d. 20 Jun 1944.

Raymond m. (1) Clara LAUSHEY.

Children:
+ 96 F i   Ruth SHEARER.

62 Monte Clair SHEARER, b. 28 Feb 1898.

Monte m. (1) Mabel WIKER.

Children:
   97 F i   Carolyn SHEARER m. (1) Jay R. WALTERS.

              Children: James, Beverly and John WALTERS.

+ 98 M ii   Gordon S. SHEARER.

64 Frederick Clair McClain SHEARER

Frederick m. Kathryn BAXTER.

Children:
+   99F i   Betty June SHEARER.
   100M ii   Clair McClain SHEARER m. Joan SEIGFRIED.

71 Lyman Bruce SHEARER, b. 9 Jun 1896.

Lyman m. Mary McElhaney McMULLEN 29 Mar 1916. Mary b.
3 Jun 1899.

Lyman Bruce SHEARER retired in May 1961 after teaching
school for 43 years. He and his wife celebrated their
65th Wedding Anniversary in 1981.

Children:
   101F i   Louise Margaret SHEARER, b. 5 May
              1917.

              Louise m. Irwin Snively SHOOP 19 May 1934.
              Irwin, b. 2 Feb 1916.

Children:
Patricia, Bonnie, Larry, Ray and Carol
SHOOP.

102F   ii   Miriam Mae SHEARER, b. 23 Jul
1919.
Miriam m. (1) Freeburn Paul LOVE 23 Dec
1939.

Children:
Marlene, Norman and Elaine LOVE.

103F   iii   Marjorie Catherine SHEARER.
+ 104M   iv   Clair Lorraine SHEARER.
105F   v   Lois Annalee SHEARER, b. 13 Jan
1931.

Lois m. (1) William Solomon WERT 7 Nov 1953.
William, b. 10 May 1934.
Children:
Susan, Constance and Sallie WERT.

+ 106 M   vi   Richard Darwin SHEARER.

72 Frederick Carl SHEARER, b. 22 Apr 1900; d. 6 Dec 1971.

Frederick m. (1) Evelyn THATCHER, Evelyn, b. 1902.

Children:
107 M   i   Harold SHEARER, b. 1922; d. 1928.
108 F   ii   Martha SHEARER, b. 1930; d. 1930.

80 Leroy SHEARER, b. 27 Sep 1899.

Leroy m. (1) Mary BRIGGS 5 Nov 1921. Mary, b. 9 Jun
1899.

Leroy retired from Pennelec in 1965 after 42 years of
service.

Children:
+ 109 F   i   Rosalyn SHEARER.
+ 110 F   ii   Anna Mae SHEARER.

81 Harvey Donald SHEARER, b. 25 Nov 1901.

Harvey m. (1) Nina GARDINER, Washington, NJ. Nina, b.
11 Oct 1901; d. 18 Apr 1976.

Children:
+ 111F i   Doris Jean SHEARER.
+ 112M ii   Harvey Donald Jr. SHEARER.

```
+  113M iii   William Linden SHEARER.
+  114M iv    Richard Lee SHEARER.
   115M v     Kenneth Lee SHEARER, b. 12 Apr 1936.
               Kenneth m. Anna PIPER 12 Jul 1956.

+  116F vi    Gloria SHEARER.
+  117F vii   Twila Dawn SHEARER.
   118F viii  Linda SHEARER (adopted), b. 20 Sep 1955.
```

82 Earl James SHEARER, b. 6 Aug 1902.

Earl m. (1) Ann Margaret MILLER 24 Apr 1937 at York, PA. Ann, b. 3 Mar 1911.
    Earl and Ann were married by Rev. Ralph W. Linn, formerly of Scotland Lutheran Church. They were members of King Street United Brethren Church. They went to housekeeping on the Warm Spring Road in Chambersburg area, later moved to Stoufferstown. In 1971 they resided in the MILLER home estate. Mr. Shearer retired as Star Route Mail Carrier after 28 years of service. His route was from Chambersburg to McConnelsburg.

```
Children:
+  119F i    Lois Elaine SHEARER.
   120F ii   Margaret Ann SHEARER, b. 6 Nov 1941.

               Margaret m. (1) Duwayne McKerrick PATRICK 6
               Jun 1964, Chambersburg, PA. Duwayne, b. 6
               Nov 1944. They were married by Rev. Paul
               Baker, King St. United Brethren Church. They
               owned their own home and lived at R.R.1 Cold
               Spring Road, Fayetteville, PA.
                  Margaret worked at Stanley Co. Duwayne
               spent two years in the Army, including tour
               of Vietnam. His Civilian Occupation was a
               mechanic at Mack Truck, Inc., Hagerstown,
               PA.
```

FIFTH GENERATION

96 Ruth SHEARER, b. 23 Dec 1919, Lancaster, PA.

Ruth m. Harrison Lang RODGERS.

```
Children:
   121F i    Judith Ann RODGERS
               Judith m. (1) Ronald R. KNIGHT.
   122F ii   Sharyn Lang RODGERS m. (1) Robert E. HAUSEN.
   123M iii  Timothy Lang RODGERS
```

98 Gordon S. SHEARER m. Mary SWARTZ.

Children:
    124F i   Stephanie SHEARER.
    125F ii   Jennifer Lee SHEARER.

99 Betty June SHEARER m. (1) Carl SCHULTZE.

Children:
    126F i   Karen Lee SCHULTZE.
    127F ii   Martha Lynn SCHULTZE.
    128M iii Mark Edward SCHULTZE.
    129M iv   Todd Andrew SCULTZE.

103   Marjorie Catherine SHEARER, b. 28 Aug 1921.

    Marjorie m. (1) Robert B. HENRY 8 Feb 1946.
    Robert, b. 15 Jul 1925.

Children:
    130M i   James Robert HENRY, b. 23 Feb 1947.

              James m. (1) Rosalie HAMMING 15 Dec 1968.

    131F ii   Andrea Gail HENRY, b. 27 Jul 1956.

              Andrea m. (1) Richard Charles SHILEY 13 May
              1978. Richard, b. 3 Oct 1957.

    132F iii Paula Jean HENRY, b. 1 May 1957.

              Paula m. (1) Douglas Brent LAUVER 15 Jul
              1978. Douglas, b. 16 Oct 1957.

    133F iv   Jill Kathleen HENRY, b. 17 Jan 1963.

104   Clair Lorraine SHEARER, b. 20 Jul 1925.

    Clair m. (1) Dorothy ROBINSON 23 Nov 1949. Dorothy,
    b. 13 Dec 1925.

Children:
    134M i   Garry James SHEARER, b. 24 Jun 1951.

              Garry m. (1) Nancy KITZMILLER 23 Sep 1972;
              they divorced. Nancy, b. 9 Dec 1952.

              Garry m. (2) Sue Lease STILES 9 Aug 1980.
              Sue, b. 2 Oct 1954. They lived at 132 N.
              32nd St., Camp Hill, PA.

```
+    135M  ii    Alan Clair SHEARER.
     136F  iii   Lori Jo SHEARER, b. 1 Oct 1960.  Lori
                 attended Bloomsburg State College and
                 majored in nursing.
                 (Information on Bruce SHEARER Family was
                 furnished by Mr. and Mrs. Robert B. HENRY,
                 4 Mar 1981 to P.L. HAMMOND) (Philip)
```

106   Richard Darwin SHEARER, b. 26 Mar 1939.

Richard m. Nancy L. RICE 16 Jul 1960. Nancy, b. 14
Apr 1943.

Children:
```
     137M  i     Jeffrey Nathaniel SHEARER, b. 15 Aug 1961.

                 Jeffrey m. (1) Rena Kay JONES 20 Dec 1980.
                 Rena, b. 20 Aug 1960.

     138M  ii    Richard Todd SHEARER, b. 16 Oct 1962.
     139F  iii   Wendy Nannette SHEARER, b. 18 May 1965.
     140M  iv    Matthew Curtis SHEARER, b. 6 Feb 1971.
```

109   Rosalyn SHEARER, b. Oct 1922.

Rosalyn m. (1) Wilmer COWDEN 4 Oct 1947, Hagerstown,
MD. Wilmer b. 14 Apr 1916; d. 6 Nov 1980. They lived
at 133 East King St., Shippensburg, PA in 1980.

Children:
```
     141F  i     Marilyn Ann COWDEN, b. 28 Aug 1952.

                 Marilyn m. (1) Michael OSTRA 24 Dec 1972.
                 Michael, b. 3 Dec 1950.
```

110   Anna Mae SHEARER, b. 29 Jul 1928.

Anna m. (1) Charles OTT 8 Oct 1947, Shippensburg, PA.
Charles b. 16 Sep 1928.

Children:
```
     142F  i     Nancy Louise OTT, b. 13 May 1949.  It was
                 Friday.
                 Nancy m. (1) Joe DUGAS 23 Nov 1975.  Joe b.
                 27 Oct 1942.
```

Anna m. (2) George RHINEHART 4 Feb 1956, Shippensburg,
PA. George, b. 19 Dec 1922.

Children:
```
     143 M     ii      George L. RHINEHART.
```

111   Doris Jean SHEARER, b. 21 Jun 1929.

   Doris m. (1) Richard Paul WARREN 8 Aug 1954, Newville,
   PA.

Children:
   144F i   Melinda Sue WARREN, b. 17 May 1956.

              Melinda m. (1) Larry LANDIS.

112   Harvey Donald Jr. SHEARER b. 24 Dec 1931.

   Harvey m. (1) Helen C. HUTCHINSON 24 Sep 1955,
   Orrstown, PA. They lived on Route 11, Shippensburg,
   PA.

Children:
   145M i   Harvey Donald III SHEARER, b. 27 Aug 1956.
   146F ii   Susan Lynn SHEARER, b. 30 Oct 1958.
   147F iii   Betsy Jo SHEARER, b. 25 Jan 1962.

113   William Linden SHEARER, b. 10 May 1933.

   William m. (1) Jo Anne M. WEARY 1 Feb 1956.
   Address: Chestnut St., Newville, PA in 1980.

Children:
   148M i   William Linden Jr. SHEARER, b. 28 Jul 1957.
 + 149M ii   Jeffrey Weary SHEARER.
   150F iii   Tracey Ann SHEARER, b. 16 May 1960.
   151F iv   Valerie Jo Anne SHEARER, b. 13 Dec 1969.

114   Richard Lee SHEARER, b. 10 Nov 1934.

   Richard m. (1) Joyce (_____) Jul 1955.

Children:
   152F i   (_____) SHEARER.

   Richard Lee SHEARER m. (2) Carolyn HOCKENBERRY.

Children:
   153M ii   Edward SHEARER.
   154M iii   Robert SHEARER.

   Richard Lee SHEARER m. (3) Nancy FREY.

Children:
   155M iv   Andrew B. SHEARER, b. 1963.
   156F v   Neidi Jo SHEARER, b. Jul 1967.

116   Gloria SHEARER, b. 29 May 1939.

Gloria m. (1) Richard Ellis WILLIAMS 22 Dec 1957.

Children:
    157M i   Richard Alan WILLIAMS, b. 19 Aug 1960.
    158F ii   Vickie Mae WILLIAMS, b. 2 Apr 1962.
    159F iii Jody Kay WILLIAMS, b. 26 May 1964.

117   Twila Dawn SHEARER, b. 9 Dec 1943.

Twila m. (1) Donald WINTERS.

Children:
    160M i   Jacob WINTERS.
    161F ii   Joyann WINTERS.

119   Lois Elaine SHEARER, b. 1 Mar 1938.

Lois m. (1) George Edward MACHAL 27 Apr 1957. George
son of Edward MACHAL and Edna SHOEMAKER was b. 23 Dec
1935.
        Lois and George were married by Bishop Clyde W.
Meadows,   King   St.   United   Brethren   Church,
Chambersburg, PA.

        The Machals have been stationed in North and
South Carolina, Tennessee, New York, Virginia and
Kanache Bay, Oahee, Hawaii. Overseas tours were Japan
and DaNang, South VietNam. George was a Gunnery/Sgt,
USMC for twenty years.

Children:
    162F i   Nina Marie MACHAL, b. 4 Feb 1958.

                    SIXTH GENERATION

135   Alan Clair SHEARER, b. 14 Jun 1959.

Alan m. (1) Pamela BARRETT 13 Jul 1975; they divorced
in 1978. Pamela later remarried. She and her next
husband legally adopted Kimberly Ann.

Children:
    163F i   Kimberly Ann SHEARER, b. 15 Dec 1975.

Alan m. (2) Diane ANDERSON 29 Sep 1979. Diane, b. 27
Dec 1959. Their address: RD 1, Newville, PA.

Children:
    164F ii   Heidi Diane SHEARER, b. 2 Dec 1980.

149   Jeffrey Weary SHEARER, b. 1 Jan 1959.

    Jeffrey m. (1) Terry Elizabeth WEBBER 29 Nov 1980.
Children:
    165M i   Matthew Scott SHEARER, b. 28 Apr 1981.

- - - - - - - - - - - - - - - - - -

DESCENDANTS OF JOSEPH DEVOR, SON OF JESSE

FIRST GENERATION

1   Joseph DEVOR, b. 19 May 1820, Spring Run, Franklin
    Co., PA; d. 1892; bur. Doylesburg, PA.

    Joseph m. (1) Maria SHETLER abe. 1848.
        They lived at Doylesburg, Path Valley, Franklin
    Co., PA.

Children:
    2 F   i   Jane DEVOR.
    3 F   ii   Annie DEVOR.
+   4 M   iii   Martin G. DEVOR.
    5 U   iv   (_____) DEVOR.

    Joseph m. (2) Elizabeth PIPER.

SECOND GENERATION

4   Martin G. DEVOR, b. 1853; d. 1935, Doylesburg, PA.
        Martin was crippled.   (Corwin)

    Martin m. (1) Mary "Molly" FAGAN.   Mary, b. 1870; d.
    1931 Doylesburg, PA.

Children:
    6 M   i   Jesse DEVOR.
+   7 F   ii   Elizabeth J. DEVOR.

THIRD GENERATION

7   Elizabeth J. DEVOR, b. Aug 1910.

    Elizabeth m. (1) J. Ray LAUTHERS.   Ray, son of John
    LAUTHERS and Myrtle C. CLUGSTON, b. 5 Jan 1905; d. 27
    Nov 1978.
        Ray died of a heart attack while hunting deer.

Children:
    8 M   i   Roger J. LAUTHERS, b. 30 Mar 1939; d. 18 Nov
                1972.

DESCENDANTS OF JAMES H. DEVOR, SON OF JESSE

FIRST GENERATION

1   James H. DEVOR, b. 7 Nov 1822, Spring Run, Franklin
    Co., PA; d. 1 Feb 1888; bur. Pine Grove Cemetery,
    Tuscarora Valley, PA.

    James m. (1) Malinda Jane PETERSON.

Children:
    2 F   i   Mary DEVOR.   She married (_____) DRAKE, a
                farmer.

- - - - - - - - - - - - - - - - - - - -

DESCENDANTS OF DAVID H. DEVOR, SON OF JESSE

FIRST GENERATION

1   David H. DEVOR, b. 1 Feb 1825, Spring Run, Franklin
    Co., PA; d. 1906, near Pawnee City, Pawnee Co., NE;
    bur. Burchard, Pawnee Co., NE.

    David m. (1) Mary Ann LAIRD 1849.
        David and Mary Ann homesteaded in southeast
    Nebraska and reared their family at Pawnee City.
    (Cora)

Children:
+   2 F   i   Elizabeth Laird "Lizzie" DEVOR.
+   3 F   ii   Rachel Fiester DEVOR.
+   4 F   iii   John William DEVOR.
+   5 M   iv   Joseph Henry DEVOR.
+   6 F   v   Mary "Mollie" DEVOR.

    David m. (2) Fannie BATES. Fannie b. London, England.

Children:
+   7 M   vi   Frank S. DEVOR.

2   Elizabeth Laird "Lizzie" DEVOR, b. 3 Mar 1851,
Franklin Co., PA.

    Elizabeth m. (1) John Blaine TALLMAN 3 Mar 1870,
Pawnee City, Pawnee Co., NE.

Children:
    8 F   i   Lulu TALLMAN.
    9 F   ii   Mae TALLMAN.
    10 F iii   (_____) TALLMAN.

3   Rachel Fiester DEVOR, b. 21 Jun 1855, Woodhull, Henry
    Co., IL.

    Rachel m. (1) Abraham "Abe" Lyons GILMORE 4 Oct 1876,
Pawnee City, Pawnee Co., NE.

        They lived at Chadron, NE. Moved to Soldier, ID.

Children:
+   11 F i   Maude GILMORE.
    12 M ii   Floyd GILMORE.
    13 M iii   Guy GILMORE, b. 1883. Has daughter Rachael.
    14 M iv   David GILMORE, he m. (1) (_____).
    15 F v   Blanche GILMORE m. (1) Charles WOODY.
                They lived at Hagerman, ID.

    16 F vi   Pearl GILMORE, b. 1888.
                Pearl m. (1) (-----) WOLVINGTON.
                They lived at Rushville, NE.

    17 F vii   Julia GILMORE m. Reuben WOODY.
                They lived at Hagerman, ID.

    18 F viii Fay GILMORE, blue baby, died in infancy.

4   John William DEVOR, b. 12 Feb 1857, Woodhull, Henry
    Co., IL; d. 7 Mar 1940, McPherson, McPherson Co., KS;
    bur. McPherson, McPherson Co., KS

    John m. (1) Rhoda Ann "Rhodie" GILMORE 18 Oct 1879.
Rhoda, dau. of David GILMORE and Sarah HIGANBOTHAN, b.
24 Feb 1861, Logan Co., OH; d. 29 Oct 1939, McPherson,
McPherson Co., KS; bur., McPherson, McPherson Co., KS.
    John was a teacher and farmer. Rhoda was a laundress
and he helped her with the laundry business in Geary, OK,
in 1900.

They were Free Methodists. They lived at various places, Henry Co., IL; Pawnee Co., NE; Geary, Blaine Co., OK; and McPherson, McPherson Co., KS. (Zella)

In 1918, when his granddaughter, Zella DEVOR, was just eleven John William came to live with them at Beaver Co., OK. He taught school there one year and told Zella stories about the family. He told her that William Penn was a friend of a Devor and gave him a large tract of land in Pennsylvania.

Years later Zella visited Corwin Johnston who had researched the Devor family and he told her that John Devor obtained 200 acres in PA and was probably the father of Joseph DEVOR, her great great grandfather. It was later noted that Corwin could not prove the connection.

Children:
+ 19 M i   Arthur Abraham DEVOR.
+ 20 M ii   Cecil Hart DEVOR.
  21 M iii   John Wesley DEVOR, b. about 1901; d. before 7 Jan 1992.

> John m. Blanche BATCHILDER.
> John Wesley was a Professor at Asbury College at Wilmore, Kentucky and also at American U. of Washington D.C. He retired to California in 1975. According to his niece, Zella Devor Forrester in a letter dated Jan 7, 1992, John died of cancer.

5   Joseph Henry DEVOR, b. 5 Jun 1859, Gary, IL; d. 12 May 1938, Walterville, Lane Co., OR.

Joseph m. (1) Sabina Jane "Bina" SPRACKLIN 2 Jul 1881, Pawnee City, Pawnee, NE. Sabina, dau. of Peter "Pete" SPRACKLIN and Catherine "Kate" RUSSELL, b. 5 May 1860; d. 21 Mar 1936, Walterville, Lane Co., OR.

Joseph and Sabina homesteaded at Chadron, NE. They built a log house on their 160 acres where their first three children, Ralph, Helen and Claude, were born. The log house was followed by a frame house.

When Helen, Claude and Opal attended school in Nebraska they had to walk a half mile two months in the fall and three months in the spring. In Nebraska the teacher boarded around from family to family. Sabina was familiar with this system as she had taught several terms prior to her marriage and had received the large salary of $20 a month.

The year 1897 was a big one for the Devors. The family bought a fine new organ, one of few in the community and Cora was born on the fourth of December.

By 1897 the Devors had experienced temperatures of 50 degrees below zero and began to think of going to Oregon, the land of milk and honey where drought, crop failures, blizzards, grasshoppers and rattlesnakes were unknown.

Sixteen families of the community prepared to migrate to Oregon. They sold their homes and farm animals for what they could get for them and kept their horses to pull the wagons.

On 7 June 1899 the families left for the promised land. The Devors had a two-seated buggy "Hack" and a wagon full of supplies. The families chartered a freight car to carry their furniture, including the Devor's new organ that was in the family until 1990.

It took three months to reach Walterville, the home of relatives. Hop picking at Smeads yards was in full swing and the family camped with relatives and picked hops for the rest of the season. There was lots of fruit in the area and the weary travelers could pick all they wanted.

The Devors settled at Walterville, OR where Joseph was Justice of the Peace. They helped to establish the Walterville Presbyterian Church.

In Walterville, Sabina was one of the Ladies Aid members who applied for Articles of Incorporation so that the Society could own property. The Presbyterian Church built on property obtained by the Ladies Aid.

Joseph, Sabina and Cora were charter members of the Church and Joseph served on the first Board of Deacons. Joseph taught Sunday School and served as Sunday School Superintendent. Joseph and Sabina sang in the choir. (Cora)

In 1938 Joseph had cancer on his arms and in one ear. The family conferred and collected $200 for an ear operation at a sanatorium in Savannah, MO. Cora was elected to go with him. His ear was removed but the cancer got worse. (Jim Wearin)

Children:
22 M i   Ralph Winfield DEVOR, b. Sep 1882, Pawnee City, Pawnee Co., NE, d. Oct 1883, Pawnee City, Pawnee Co., NE.

23 F ii   Helen Agnes "Nellie" DEVOR, b. 29 Oct 1883, Pawnee City, Pawnee Co., NE; d. 1969.
          Helen m. (1) Merle PIERCE 1920.
             They homesteaded in the Sheridan area of Wyoming. They raised sheep and a few cows. They had three children.

24 M iii Claude Ernest DEVOR, b. 8 Oct 1884, Pawnee City, Pawnee Co., NE.; d. 1 Mar 1973,

Sheridan, WY. Claude was a cowboy and never married. He had a coal mine on his homestead.

+ 25 F iv   Opal Ruth DEVOR.
+ 26 F v   Cora Elizabeth DEVOR.
  27 M vi   Joseph Clement DEVOR, b. 22 Aug 1900, Walterville, Lane Co., OR.; d. 22 Nov 1971, Redding, CA.

6 Mary "Mollie" DEVOR, b. Pawnee City, NE.
Mary m. (1) Clarence MILES.
    They lived about 4 miles west of Pawnee City, NE. about 1900. In 1915 they were living at Long Beach, CA and visited the Wearins in Oregon. (Cora)

Children:
  28 F i   (_____) MILES, adopted.

7 Frank S. DEVOR, b. 12 Jan 1877; d. 22 Jan 1939, Seneca, KS.

Frank m. (1) Mary Jane SHAW 20 Mar 1900, Beatrice, NE., Mary, b. 25 Dec 1884; d. 14 Jan 1948, Seneca, KS.
    Cora Wearin visited them in Pawnee City in 1903. She saw them again in 1938 when she had her father at a cancer sanitorium at Savanah, Missouri. Frank died in 1939 shortly after they had visited. Corwin Johnston is our only source for the children of Frank S. DEVOR.

Children:
  29 F i   Ruemma DEVOR, b. 16 Mar 1901, Pawnee City, Pawnee Co., NE.

              Ruemma m. (1) Frank MENDENHALL. They lived in Omaha, NE.

  30 M ii   Amos F. DEVOR, b. 19 Feb 1903, Pawnee City, Pawnee Co., NE,; d. 27 Jan 1924.

  31 F iii   Marion DEVOR, b. 3 Nov 1906.
              Marion m. (1) Ted DURRYEA.

  32 F iv   Pansy DEVOR, b. 1 Jan 1909.
              Pansy m. (1) Ward GROVENBURG.

  33 F v   Hazel DEVOR, b. 28 Oct 1912.
              Hazel m. (1) Richard POTTER.
              Hazel m. (2) Merle COOK.

```
34 M vi     David DEVOR, b. 18 Jul 1914.
            David m. (1) Faye MILLER.

35 F vii    Allie DEVOR, b. 1 Dec 1917, Audubon, IA.
            Allie m. Albert WILTZ.

36 M viii   Frank DEVOR, b. 12 Jan 1920, Gearing, NE.
            Frank m. (1) Agatha (_____).
            Frank m. (2) Irene STORTZ.

37 F ix     Vivian DEVOR, b. 12 Jan 1922, Seneca, KS.
            Vivian m. John SNODGRASS.

38 F x      Betty DEVOR, b. 30 Oct 1925, Seneca, KS.
            Betty m. (1) Quentin JOHNSTON.
```

THIRD GENERATION

```
11 Maude GILMORE, b. 1878.
Maude m. (1) Jim CHALK.

Children:
39 M i      Frank CHALK, b. 1897.

Maude m. (2) Andrew HALLSTEAD.
```

        Cora Wearin said, "She married twice. Her first husband was Jim Chalk. Their child, Frank Chalk. Second husband, Andrew Hallstead. I visited her in 1903 and also about 1950 at their farm home near Chadron, NE."

```
19 Arthur Abraham DEVOR, b. 2 Sep 1880, Pawnee, NE.; d.
3 Jul 1948, Salina, Saline Co., KS, bur. McPherson,
McPherson Co., KS.

Arthur m. (1) Sarah WILKLOW.

Children:
    40 M i      Cecil Wilklow DEVOR.
+   41 M ii     Arthur William DEVOR.
    42 M iii    Howard DEVOR.
    43 F iv     Mabel DEVOR.
    44 F v      Doris Marybelle DEVOR.
    45 F vi     Jessie "Terry" DEVOR.
                Jessie m. (_____) WING and lived at Crescent
                City.
    46 F vii    Iva DEVOR.
                Iva m. (_____) BAKER and lived at Montrose,
                CO.
    47 M viii   George DEVOR.  Lived at Montrose, CO.
```

20 Cecil Hart DEVOR, b. 17 Oct 1883, Pawnee City, Pawnee
Co., NE; d. 16 Mar 1966, Salina, Salina Co., KS; bur.
28 Mar 1966, McPherson, McPherson Co., KS.

Cecil m. (1) Maude Mabel PETTIS 13 May 1905, Watonga,
OK. Maude, dau. of Lorenzo Dow "Ranny" PETTIS and
Miranda Ellen WARRINGTON, b. 25 Mar 1885, Concordia,
Cloud Co., KS; d. 9 Sep 1955, Wichita, Sedgwick Co.,
KS; bur. McPherson, McPherson Co., KS.
     Cecil was a farmer and a Free Methodist preacher.
He and Maude served congregations in rural towns in
Kansas, Oklahoma and Nebraska. (Zella)

Children:
+   48 M i   Arthur Agnew DEVOR.
+   49 F ii   Zella Ruth DEVOR
+   50 F iii   Rilla Ermina DEVOR.
+   51 M iv   Cecil Hart DEVOR, Jr.
+   52 M v   Charles Wesley DEVOR.
+   53 M vi   Joseph Eldon DEVOR.
+   54 M vii   Virgil Wayne DEVOR.
+   55 F viii Beulah Mae DEVOR.
    56 F ix   Mary Ellen DEVOR, twin, b. ca 1920, Sophia,
               Beaver Co., OK; d. 1920, Sophia, Beaver Co.,
               OK; bur. Sophia Cemetery, Beaver Co., OK.

    57 M x   John Abraham DEVOR, twin, b. ca 1920,
               Sophia, Beaver Co., OK; d. 1920, Sophia,
               Beaver Co., OK; bur., Sophia Cemetery,
               Sophia, Beaver Co., OK.

25 Opal Ruth DEVOR, b. 24 Oct 1888, Chadron, NE; d. 12
Aug 1986, Sunnyvale, CA.

Opal m. (1) Albert Knapp "Hal" JENNINGS 14 Aug 1907,
Walterville, Lane Co., OR. Hal d. 1969.

     Opal came to Oregon from Nebraska by covered
wagon at age 11. She lived at Walterville, OR and at
age 19 married Hal JENNINGS, a mail coach driver along
the Oregon coast.
     Opal was a poet and a seamstress, contributing
poems to "The Register Guard", a Eugene Oregon daily
newspaper, and making hundreds of quilts.
     After World War II she and Hal settled in
Portland, OR, where they opened their antique business
which they operated until 1965. Hal died in 1969 and
Opal moved to Sunnyvale, California to be near her
daughter Beth.

Children:
    58 F i   Ellen JENNINGS m. (1) Billy KORN.
+   59 M ii   Kenneth JENNINGS.
+   60 F iii   Beth JENNINGS.

26 Cora Elizabeth DEVOR, b. 4 Dec 1897, Chadron, NE; d.
   11 Apr 1988, at "Twilight Acres" nursing home,
   Pleasant Hill, Eugene, OR; bur., Greenwood Cemetery,
   Leaburg, OR.
        Cora's first teaching job, just after High
   School, was at Troy, Oregon. In order to get there
   she had to go by train to Pendleton, by stage coach to
   Enterprise and from there on horseback. The Troy
   school was at Denton Ridge above Troy in the valley.
   In 1995 the school was still there and so were some of
   the people with whom she had boarded.

   Cora m. Everett WEARIN 1 Sep 1920, Walterville, Lane
   Co., OR. Everett, son of M. J. WEARIN and Rosa Lee
   BYERS, b. 25 Sep 1897, Milan, KS; d. 25 Jan 1990,
   Springfield, Lane Co., OR; bur. 3 Feb 1990, Greenwood
   Cemetery, Leaburg, Lane Co., OR.
        After their marriage Cora and Everett took a
   honeymoon trip to California, then came back up the
   McKenzie by Belknap where they worked for Mr. Quimby
   who had a roadhouse. They were there about a year.
   They moved to North Bend, OR where their children,
   Lilah and Jim, were born. At the time Jim was born,
   both he and Cora contracted mumps in the hospital.
   She was entirely unable to care for her two children
   for a year. She lived with her in-laws during this
   time.
        Cora was a country news correspondent for "The
   Register Guard" and "The Springfield News" when that
   was popular years ago. She was a 4-H Club leader for
   50 years and was an avid rockhound and took 4-H
   children on many geology excursions. She taught
   elementary school at many schools in Oregon including
   Goshen, Trent, Paradise, Eden, Zion, Florence,
   Wendling and Deerhorn. After that she confined her
   teaching to the Springfield Consolidated District with
   5th grade being her specialty.
        Cora was well known for her hand-pieced quilts
   and her quilting. Cora's hobbies included collecting
   wish bones of birds and collecting buttons. Her wish
   bone hobby almost turned Everett's stomach at one
   time. He and Cora were on the beach and she found a
   dead sea gull. She took it back to their travel
   trailer, cooked it, and got the wish bone for her
   collection. She sewed thousands of buttons on cards
   in designs.

Everett was in the logging business. He was a faller and bucker in the woods for more than 40 years. He had been active in the community since 1912 when he moved to Walterville. He was also a 4-H leader and a member of the Walterville Grange #416 and the Presbyterian Church. He also loved to travel and go rock hunting.

In 1928 Everett received a piece of land and $500 from his father and built a three bedroom house on the McKenzie Highway.

Everett and Cora were rock hounds and collected stones in Eastern Oregon. Everett constructed a building next to his home to store and polish the stones and then sell to people who were attracted by his "Rock Hound Ranch" sign on the highway.

Cora was a charter member of the Walterville Presbyterian church where she played the piano and sang alto in the choir. She was an active member of the Walterville Grange.

She worked hard physically, teaching her children how to work. She taught Jim and Lilah to pick beans and other crops during the depression to earn money for their school clothes.

In her later years Cora could not walk without her metal walker and so spent many hours at her quilting frame making quilts.

For her last 5 years she was tenderly cared for by the staff at the Twilight Acres Nursing Home. Cora was the last living pioneer of the Devor family that settled in Walterville. (This Is Your Life Cora Wearin) (Anna)

Everett lived alone after Cora went to the nursing home. He also had to use a walker to get around in the house and his riding lawn mower to get around outside.

He enjoyed talking about the old days with visitors and told them how he put venison on the table during the depression, sometimes in season, and how he was baptized in the canal.

He went to a nursing home in late 1989 and died in Jan 1990. A memorial service was held Feb 3 at the McKenzie Valley Presbyterian church in Walterville with Pastor Dave VanDyke officiating. (Anna)

Children:
+ 61 F i   Lilah WEARIN.
+ 62 M ii   James Everett WEARIN.

41 Arthur William DEVOR lived at Brookings, SD after retirement. Arthur m. Miss (_____).

Children:
    63 F i   Karen DEVOR.
    64 M ii   Kenneth DEVOR.
    65 F iii   Mary DEVOR.

48 Arthur Agnew DEVOR, b. 23 May 1906, Geary, Blaine Co., OK Territory; d. Aug 1995.

Arthur Agnew m. (1) Hallie May HARRIS 3 Sep 1930, Taloga, Dewey Co., OK.
      Arthur was a farmer at Siloam Springs, AR. He retired and divided his farm among his three children.

Children:
    66 M i   Herbert DEVOR.
    67 F ii   Patricia DEVOR.
    68 M iii   Bobby DEVOR.

49 Zella Ruth DEVOR, b. 14 Sep 1907, Sophia, Beaver Co., Oklahoma Territory; d. 10 Feb 1998, Wichita, KS.
      Zella Ruth DEVOR, daughter of Cecil Hart DEVOR was born 2 months and 2 days before Oklahoma became a state.
      Zella's father encouraged her interest in genealogy. When she was young he took her to Pawnee City, NE and showed her his birthplace and the school that he had attended. He also showed her the house where her great grandfather had lived and the cemetery where he is buried.
      When Zella was eleven her grandfather, John William DEVOR, came to live with them at Beaver Co., OK. He taught school there one year and told Zella stories about the family. He told her that William Penn was a friend of a DEVOR and gave him a large tract of land in Pennsylvania.
      Years later she visited Corwin Johnston who had researched the Devor family and he told her that John DEVOR obtained 200 acres in PA and was probably the father of Joseph DEVOR, her great great grandfather.

Zella m. (1) Russell Newton FORRESTER 24 Nov 1927, Cedarville, Woodward Co., OK. Russell, son of Mr. FORRESTER and Charlotte Elizabeth JESSIE, b. 17 Jan 1907, Chester, OK; d. 16 Oct 1992, Wichita, KS.
      Russell graduated from Seiling OK High School as did Zella. His hobbies were gardening, photography and working in his shop. He and Zella attended a

camera club. Upon retirement Russell bought a house trailer and he and Zella traveled five months each year. When they settled down in Wichita, KS they had many colored slides to show.

Zella had a strong interest in her church. She taught the primary grades in Sunday School for 25 years and had offices in the Women's Mission Society. She also served as Sunday School Secretary. (Zella)

Zella lived in Wichita, KS and died there after a series of minor strokes. (Beulah)

Children:
69 M i   Rene Arley FORRESTER, b. 6 Nov 1931, Chester, OK. Rene has stayed single and worked at electronic design and lived at home.

+ 70 M ii   Donald Lee FORRESTER.

50 Rilla Ermina DEVOR, b. 22 Nov 1908, Self's Ranch, SW of Geary, Blaine Co., OK.
Rilla m. (1) Clarence HAMILTON.
Rilla was a school teacher. She suffered from a bad heart as did her brothers Charles, Eldon and Cecil. (Zella)

Children:
71 F i   Yvonne HAMILTON, b. 1933.
72 M ii   Eudene HAMILTON, b. abe 1937.

51 Cecil Hart DEVOR Jr., b. 23 Jun 1910, Self's Ranch, SW of Geary, Blaine Co., OK; d. bef 7 Jan 1992, Wichita, KS.

Cecil m. (1) Beulah (_____).

Children:
73 M i   Marion DEVOR.
74 F ii   Kathy DEVOR m. (1) David WILSON.

52 Charles Wesley DEVOR, b. 31 Oct 1912.
Charles m. Miss (_____).

Children:
75 F i   Charleen DEVOR m. (1) James COURSON.

53 Joseph Eldon DEVOR, b. 15 Apr 1914, Sophia, Beaver Co., OK: d. 10 May 1983, McPherson, McPherson Co., KS; bur. 14 May 1983, McPherson, McPherson Co., KS.

Joseph m. (1) Alice Noyes EPPERSON.
        Joseph was born near Sophia in a sod house on the
Sweet farm which Cecil had purchased. He was a
minister in the Free Methodist Church and a teacher of
science and math. He had a fine bass voice and sang
in the choir. His death was caused by a heart attack.

Children:
    76 F i   Velma Jean DEVOR.
+   77 F ii   Mary Alice DEVOR.

54 Virgil Wayne DEVOR, b. 19 Oct 1915, Sophia, Beaver
    Co., OK; d. 19 Jul 1983.

    Virgil m. (1) Irline King.
        Virgil was a minister. He died of cancer. His
    first wife, Irline, died of cancer about 1966.
    (Zella)

Children:
    78 F i   Rosalie DEVOR.
    79 M ii   Victor DEVOR.
    80 F iii   Mary Ann DEVOR.
+   81 M iv   Jerel DEVOR.

    Virgil m. (2) Hazel (_____).

55 Beulah Mae DEVOR b. Apr 1917.
    Beulah m. (1) Paul MASON. They divorced in 1948.

Children:
    82 M i   Louis Mason b. 1939 m. (1) Suzanne GIERLICH
+   83 M ii   Rex MASON

    Beulah m. (2) Warner SPANN 1956, he d. 1993.

59 Kenneth JENNINGS m. (1) Ethel THIENES.

Children:
    84 M i   Chuck JENNINGS.

60 Beth JENNINGS m. (1) Steve ERICKSON.

Children:
    85 F i   Stephanie ERICKSON.

61 Lilah WEARIN, b. 24 Jan 1924, North Bend, OR.

    Lilah m. (1) Oliver Cecil JOHNSON 29 Jun 1941,
    Walterville, Lane Co., OR. Oliver, son of Edwin
    JOHNSON and Ruth THOMPSON, b. 13 Mar 1916, Sifton, WA;
    d. 8 Aug 1989, McKenzie Willamette Hospital,

Springfield, OR; bur. 8 Aug 1989, Memorial Gardens Mausoleum, Springfield, Lane Co., OR. Memorial services were held at 10 am, Sat. Aug. 12 at McKenzie Valley Presbyterian Church with Rev. David Van Dyke officiating. Private entombment was held at Springfield Memorial Gardens Mausoleum, Hillside South Chapel Top Level #2, 7305 Main St.

Cecil had lived in the Lane County area and worked in the logging industry most of his life. Before retiring he worked as a diesel truck mechanic. An avid citizen's band operator, Johnson was affectionately known up and down the McKenzie River as "Greasy Belly". He belonged to the Lower McKenzie Neighborhood Watch. Before his many serious illnesses, he enjoyed yard work, hunting and fishing. (Lilah)

Lilah retired as an Avon Products sales person and lived in Springfield. In 1994 Lilah had a stroke while in the hospital after an operation for a knee replacement. She has been able to hear and understand but cannot talk. She had been very helpful in providing family genealogy.

She lives with her daughter, Kay and Kay's husband, Edward J. Van Houton. They have been teaching her to do many things. She bowls, puts puzzles together and makes beaded necklaces.

Children:
+   86 M i   Wayne Carrol JOHNSON.
+   87 F ii   Vivian Kay JOHNSON.
+   88 M iii   Steven Michael JOHNSON.

62 James Everett WEARIN, b. 21 Feb 1926, North Bend, OR. James lived in North Bend, OR for two years and then moved to Walterville. He attended Deerhorn grade school. His teacher liked to play softball so he taught the boys of the school and their team won the Lane County Championship three years. After graduation from grade school those students were bussed to Springfield High School where, besides school work, James played football.

Jim was drafted into the army and took basic training at Fort Riley, KS. In 1944 he went overseas with the First Armored Division landing at Naples, Italy. Two weeks later they were shipped to north of Rome and went up to Northern Italy. At the end of the war he returned home and worked in the logging industry for 42 years. He retired in 1987 and enjoys working in his yard and fishing. (James Wearin)

James m. (1) Betty Lou (LEMAZZI) DICK 12 May 1949.
Betty d. 1991. After Betty Lou and Jim were married,
he adopted her daughter Shannon DICK in 1953.

Children:
    89 F i   Shannon Lee WEARIN, adopted
    90 M ii   Jamie Everett WEARIN

James m. (2) Marlene KITAJCHUK in 1992, Portland, OR.
They were married at the very nice little Oak Pioneer
Church in Portland, OR. By this marriage James has
three step daughters, and four grandchildren.

Children:
+   91 F iii   Laura KITAJCHUK.
+   92 F iv   Valerie KITAJCHUK.
+   93 F v   Marla KITAJCHUK.

70 Donald Lee FORRESTER, b. 26 Apr 1934, Chester, OK.
   Donald m. (1) Joan BRADY 22 Nov 1957, Wichita, KS;

Children:
    94 F i   Lisa Gay FORRESTER, b. Jan 1959, Wichita,
               KS.
               Lisa m. (1) Mark NOLAND.

+   95 M ii   Scott Alan FORRESTER, b. 8 Oct 1961 Wichita,
               KS
               Scott m. (1) Susie (_____).

   Donald m. (2) Helen GOBEN 12 Sep 1975.

77 Mary Alice DEVOR   m. (1) Richard D. "Dick" DICKINSON.
      Dick was a teacher, but has taken up appraisal of
   real estate. (Zella)

Children:
    96 M i   Richard Duane "Rick" DICKINSON II, b. 1969.
               Richard m. (1) Renee GOULD.

81 Jerel DEVOR.   m. (1) Nieta (_____).

Children:
    97 M i   Bradley DEVOR, (twin), b. 1970.
    98 M ii   Craig DEVOR, (twin), b. 1970.
    99 F iii   Lori DEVOR, b. 1973.

83 Rex MASON, b. 1947 m. (1) Lucy TELSHAW.

Children:
    100F i   Amber MASON.
    101M ii   Erin MASON.

86 Wayne Carrol JOHNSON, b. 21 Oct 1945, Eugene, Lane
Co., OR.
  He lived at Coquille, Or., was in the Army for 5
years with the German Occupation Forces. He was the
foreman for Aspland Tree Trimming Service, and thinks
he's God's gift to women. Family calls him the Great
White Hunter because he's always out after trophies.
(Lilah)

Wayne m. (1) Melva WOODS 1 Apr 1971, Springfield, Lane
Co., Or; they divorced.

Children:
+ 102F i   Jody Carrol JOHNSON, b. 24 Jan 1971.
  103M ii Donald Wayne JOHNSON, b. 10 Oct 1972,
       Springfield, Lane Co., OR.
         He loved sports and did especially well
       in baseball. He was a good goofer-offer and
       now is a good worker. (Lilah)

87 Vivian Kay JOHNSON m. (1) Jack DAVIS 1969, Vancouver,
WA. They lived in Springfield, OR.

Children:
  104F i   Susan Leann DAVIS, b. 9 Feb 1971, Portland,
       Multnomah Co., OR. Artistically talented.

Vivian Kay m. (2) Gerald Clair ROBBERSON Nov 1964,
Albany, Linn Co, Or. They divorced. Gerald b. Nov
1936, OR; d. Apr 1985, Sacred Heart Hosp., Eugene,
Lane Co., OR; cremated and buried at Fall Creek, OR.
His mother's name was Blanche ROBBERSON DAVIS.
(Lilah)

Children:
  105M ii Michael Scott ROBBERSON, b. 10 Feb 1965,
       Sacred Heart Hosp. Eugene, Lane Co., OR.
         He was a hellion when little but has
       grown up to be decent says his grandmother.
       He's a dog lover. Occupation: Logger,
       Landscaper. (Lilah)

+ 106F iii Kimberly Dawn ROBBERSON b. 20 Jan 1967,
       Sacred Heart Hospital, Eugene, Lane Co., OR.

  107M iv Richard Wayne ROBBERSON b. 3 Mar 1968,
       Portland, Multnomah Co., OR.

       Richard m. (1) (_____).

Vivian Kay m. (3) Edward J. VAN HOUTON.

88 Steven Michael JOHNSON.

   Steven m. (1) Tammy NEILSON 15 Jun 1985, Reno, NV.
   Tammy, b. 1 Jun 1963, Astoria, OR.
        She's a good cook and mother.

Children:
   108F i   Corali JOHNSON, b. 12 Sep 1986, Astoria, OR;
               chr. Aug 1990, Astoria, OR.
               Corali was christened in Catholic Church.
               She is going to a school for gifted
               children. (Lilah)

89 Shannon Lee WEARIN, b. 1 Aug 1942.
   Shannon m. (1) Jim KEENE 1972. Jim, b. 3 Jan 1942.

Children:
   109F i   Mindy WEARIN

90 Jamie Everett WEARIN, b. 1956.

   Jamie m. (1) Jody GILMORE 14 Feb 1975.

Children:
   110M i   Jason WEARIN, b. 1 Apr 1976.
               Jason m. (1) Jenny CORNETT 1996.

   111F ii   Joy WEARIN, b. 21 Oct 1978.

91 Laura KITAJCHUK m. (1) Herman CORTEZ.

Children:
   112M i   Nathan CORTEZ.

92 Valerie KITAJCHUK m. Bret PHILLIPS.

Children:
   113M i   Branden PHILLIPS.
   114F ii   Jenai PHILLIPS.

93 Marla KITAJCHUK m. (1) Craig HEIM.

Children:
   115F i   Britt May HEIM.

                    SIXTH GENERATION

95 Scott Alan FORRESTER, b. 8 Oct 1961, Wichita, KS.
   Scott m. (1) Susie (_____).

Children:
116F i   Kimberlie Kameia FORRESTER, b. 23 Jan 1993.

102   Jody Carrol JOHNSON, b. 24 Jan 1971, Springfield,
Lane Co., Or.
Jody m. (1) (_____).
        Jody excelled in baseball when in school. She
practically raised her little brother. She was born
on the birthday of her grandmother, Lilah Wearin
JOHNSON.

117M i   Ronald Sather JOHNSON, b. 15 Apr 1987,
           Springfield, Lane Co., Or.
118M ii   Alex Wayne Sather JOHNSON, b. Jun 1988,
           Springfield, Lane Co., OR.
119M iii   Richard Sather JOHNSON, b. Nov 1989,
           Lebanon, Linn Co., OR.

106   Kimberly Dawn ROBBERSON, b. 20 Jan 1967, Sacred
Heart Hospital, Eugene, Lane Co., OR.

Kimberly m. (1) David GLANDER Aug 1987, Los Angeles,
CA. He was excellent at sail boating and worked for
King Design, Awnings.
        Kimberly went to California and modeled clothes.
Lives in Springfield, OR. Works as a sales lady at
Valley River Mall. (Lilah)

Children:
120M i   Luke GLANDER, b. 5 Aug 1989, Sacred Heart
           Hospital, Eugene, Lane Co., OR.
               He's a really smart great grandson.
           (Lilah)

107   Richard Wayne ROBBERSON, b. 3 Mar 1968, Portland,
Multnomah Co., OR.
Richard m. (1) Pamela (_____)

121F i   Keerah Yvonne ROBBERSON, b. 7 Aug 1990,
           Sacred Heart Hospital, Eugene, Lane Co., OR.

DESCENDANTS OF JACOB J. DEVOR, SON OF JESSE

1 Jacob J. DEVOR, b. 16 May 1827, Spring Run, Franklin Co., PA; d. 26 Jun 1899, Spring Run, Franklin Co., PA; bur. Spring Run, Franklin Co., PA.

Jacob m. (1) Elizabeth BRINLEY 1 Mar 1849, Spring Run, Franklin Co., PA. Elizabeth, dau. of Jacob BRINLEY and Catharine "Kitty" CLIPPINGER, b. 9 Feb 1831; d. 21 Apr 1888, near Spring Run, Franklin Co., PA.
    Elizabeth's great grandparents were Jacob BRINDLEY and Eva HOUCK who came to America. Her grand parents were Michael BRINDLEY and Margaret (_____). Jacob Devor was baptized and married by Rev. Amos A. McGinley to Elizabeth Brinley.
    Jacob started life as a blacksmith in the village of Spring Run, but gave up his trade for the home farm. Under his ownership, frame buildings were erected. For many years he was a trustee of the Presbyterian Church at Spring Run. In old age he erected a home in Spring Run and retired. All biographical information about Jacob Devor and his family is from Corwin Johnson unless otherwise marked.

Children:
+ 2 F   i   Margaret Ellen DEVOR.
+ 3 M   ii   Rev. William Mackey DEVOR.
+ 4 F   iii Mary Elizabeth DEVOR.
   5 F   iv   Serepta Jane DEVOR, b. 28 Feb 1857, Spring Run, Franklin Co., PA; d. 19 Oct 1886, Haynesville, Pratt Co., KS; bur. Haynesville, Pratt Co., KS.

            Serepta m. (1) Daniel W. HAYNES 22 Feb 1886, Near Spring Run, Franklin Co., PA.
                She married Daniel Haynes, formerly of Path Valley, at the home of her father. They homesteaded at Haynesville, Kansas. Besides the farm, Mr. Haynes owned a half interest in a general store. He soon bought out his partner. They arrived at their new home on 1 Mar 1886 and started housekeeping in two rooms with new furniture and a gasoline stove.
                The evening of Oct. 18, Serepta had a headache, convulsions followed and she died the next morning. (from newspaper article pasted in the front of the Devor Bible.)

(According to Corwin Johnston, the cause of death was uremic poisoning. Corwin also reported that Daniel married again.)

+ 6 M v   Doras McGinley DEVOR.
  7 M vi   John Elmer DEVOR, b. 5 Nov 1863, Spring Run, Franklin Co., PA; d. 1 Nov 1886, Pawnee Co., NE; bur. Burchard, Pawnee Co., NE.
           John was well versed in history and government and took an active part in the campaign of General Beaver for governor in 1882. In 1885 he left Path Valley and lived and worked in Kansas and Nebraska. He became ill at the home of his cousin John William DEVOR (son of Uncle David DEVOR) and died of typhoid fever. (Devor Bible)

+ 8 F vii   Anna Susan DEVOR.
+ 9 F viii Luetta May DEVOR.
  10 F ix   Jessie Catherine DEVOR, b. 22 Jan 1871, Spring Run, Franklin Co., PA; d. 18 Jun 1936; bur. Spring Run, Franklin Co., PA.

           Jessie m. (1) J. McGinley "Max" SKINNER 30 Mar 1893. Max b. 29 Jul 1871, Dry Run, PA; d. 6 Jun 1904; bur. Spring Run, Franklin Co., PA.
           They farmed his father's farm, and then went to North Dakota to homestead. He died there on 6 Jun 1904 of heart disease.

           Jessie m. (2) Fred HEIDEMAN 13 Mar 1910. Fred, d. 20 Feb 1915, Fresno, CA.
           They went to Montana. Fred died in Fresno, CA.

           Jessie m. (3) John HAYDEN 1918.
           About 1918 she returned to PA and married John Hayden, a Civil War Veteran. They purchased the home in Spring Run that her father had built and for the remainder of their days spent summers in Spring Run and winters in Southern Pines, NC on Mr. Hayden's property. He lived to be 97.
           In her Will Jessie left her home to the Path Valley Presbyterian Church to use as a home for aged Presbyterians. The church refused the home and it was sold at private sale. However the church obtained $700 of the $2100 received for the home. The rest of the money went to Jessie's nieces and nephews.

11 F x   Huldah Eleanor DEVOR, b. 7 Jul 1872, Spring
          Run, Franklin Co., PA; d. 15 May 1936,
          Spring Run, Franklin Co., PA; bur. Spring
          Run, Franklin Co., PA.
              Huldah taught school until marriage,
          first in Pennsylvania, then in Montana.

          Huldah m. (1) Martin L. JENSEN 19 Jan 1916,
          MT. Martin d. before 1936.
          Martin Jensen preceded her in death. She
          died of cancer at the home of her sister
          Anna at Spring Run.
              Huldah left the bulk of her estate of
          $4,168 to the Spring Run Presbyterian Church
          to remodel the Brinley-Devor home that
          Jessie had donated. Huldah died before
          Jessie and did not know about the church's
          refusal of the home.
              On 5 Jun 1939 Huldah's sister Luetta
          Steele and her nephew William J. C. Devor
          filed a complaint in the Montana Court that
          the church was not entitled to money from
          Huldah's estate as it had refused the offer
          of the Brinkley-Devor home. They sued to
          have the money given to relatives. In June
          1942 Luetta Steele and Anna Johnston each
          received one sixth of the estate and the
          remaining money was divided among 17
          surviving nieces and nephews.
              Huldah also left an oil well that was
          divided among her heirs in the same manner
          as the main estate. (Corwin)

Jacob m. (2) Mariah Lettice WORK after Elizabeth's
death in 1888, she was a wonderful mother to his ten
children. Mariah was loved by Jacob's children.
Mariah survived him.
    Juanita Devor KALTENBAUGH told Mary DEVOR in May
1990 that Mariah was from Punxsutawney, PA.

                    SECOND GENERATION

2 Margaret Ellen DEVOR, b. 24 Feb 1850, Doylesburg,
Franklin Co., PA; d. 16 Feb 1923.

Margaret m. (1) Winfield Andrew WALKER 19 Jan 1875.
Winfield, b. 8 Jun 1850; d. 10 Apr 1919.
    They lived at Shirleysburg where he farmed. They
had 9 children, of which 5 died young.

Children:
+ 12 F   i   Mary Lydica WALKER.
   13 M   ii Ira Jacob WALKER, b. 21 Jan 1877,
               Shirleysburg, PA; d. 27 Apr 1881; bur.
               Shirleysburg, PA.

   14 F   iii Nora Elizabeth WALKER, b. 20 Jan 1879,
               Shirleysburg, PA; d. 22 Feb 1884; bur.
               Shirleysburg, PA.

   15 M   iv Samuel Alexander WALKER, b. 22 Aug 1880,
               Shirleysburg, PA; d. 18 Jan 1881; bur.
               Shirleysburg, PA.

   16 M   v   Jesse Winfield WALKER, b. 18 Dec 1882,
               Shirleysburg, PA; d. 11 Apr 1895; bur.
               Shirleysburg, PA. He died of diphtheria.

+ 17 F   vi Zeola Belle WALKER.
   18 M   vii John Brinley WALKER, b. 22 Nov 1887, Shirley
               Twp., Huntingdon Co., PA.

   19 M   viii Charles Devor WALKER, b. 9 May 1889,
               Shirleysburg, PA; d. 2 Apr 1895; bur.
               Shirleysburg, PA. He died of diphtheria.

   20 M   ix Newton Hayes WALKER, b. 13 Oct 1894, Shirley
               Twp., Huntingdon Co., PA.

3 Rev. William Mackey DEVOR, b. 5 Oct 1852, Spring Run,
   Franklin Co., PA; d. 9 Dec 1905, Ponca City, NE; bur.
   Ponca City, NE.

   Rev. William m. (1) Lulu L. FINNEY 10 Sep 1885,
   Leesville, OH.

        William graduated from the University of Wooster,
   Ohio and from the Western Theological Seminary,
   Allegheny, PA. He was ordained by the Presbytery of
   Wooster and installed pastor of the church at
   Perrysville, Ohio, in 1885. In May 1888 he was called
   to the pastorate of the churches of Gilgal, Rockbridge
   and Mt. Pleasant, PA in the Presbytery of Kittaning,
   Pennsylvania to which he ministered for 12 years. He
   served at Randolph and then Ponca City, Nebraska. He
   was a strong man and his sudden death from pneumonia
   was not expected. (Devor Bible)

Children:
   21 M   i   William Jay Bruce DEVOR, b. 19 Aug 1888.
   22 M   ii Galen Leslie DEVOR, b. 13 Nov 1889.

Rev. William m. (2) Helen (_____).

4   Mary Elizabeth DEVOR, b. 28 Oct 1854, Spring Run, Franklin Co., PA; d. 13 Oct 1918, Ponca City, NE.

Mary m. (1) Amos McGinley KIRKPATRICK 5 Dec 1871. Amos, b. 24 Jun 1851; d. 13 Sep 1887, Path Valley, PA; bur. Shirleysburg, PA.

Mary and Amos farmed in Cumberland Co. until his early death. She then moved to Shirleysburg with four small children and kept a boarding house. (Corwin)

Children:
23 F i   Lodemma KIRKPATRICK m. Rev C. F. BRINOR, Lodemma was a teacher. She left one son.

24 F ii   Lacea Dorcas KIRKPATRICK m. J. D. STITT. She was a teacher.

25 M iii Jacob McGinley KIRKPATRICK was a Presbyterian preacher. He left one son.

26 F iv   Luetta KIRKPATRICK m. Frank WIBLE of Three Springs. They had one son and one daughter.

6   Doras McGinley DEVOR, b. 12 Sep 1861, Spring Run, Franklin Co., PA; d. 25 May 1914, Spring Run, Franklin Co., Pa; bur. Spring Run, Franklin Co., PA.

Doras m. (1) Alice Ida HAMMOND 27 Sep 1882, Spring Run, Franklin Co., PA. Alice, dau of Martin Philip HAMMOND and Sarah Ann HAINES, b. 14 Dec 1858; d. 2 Sep 1898.
    Alice was the granddaughter of Philip HAMMOND and Mariah CRAMER, the great granddaughter of Martin Lawrence HAMMOND and Margaret BRINDLE, and the great great granddaughter of Jacob HAMMOND, the pioneer from Germany.
    Alice died suddenly at the age of 39. The family had only one small picture of her. Doras had a traveling artist make an 11"x14" copy of it which today is in the possession of her granddaughter Anna Grosvenor. After her death, Doras took a child to town with him on each trip until he had pictures of each one. (Carrie)
    Doras was a farmer. When his father died Doras and his brother William M. Devor were executors of his Will. The executors presented a petition to the Orphans Court of Franklin Co. PA asking for the estate to be sold so that Jacob's debts could be paid. The court granted permission for the sale and gave Doras

permission to bid on the estate. Doras made the successful bid and received the deed in May 1901 for a payment of $2,229.35.

Doras operated the farm and a saw mill until 1910 when he sold the farm and moved into Spring Run. In 1908 he had a stroke and suffered for six years from paralysis from which he never recovered. (Mary Takach Devor)

Children:
27 M i   John Elmer DEVOR, b. 19 Nov 1884, Spring Run Franklin Co., PA; d. 31 Aug 1890, Spring Run, Franklin Co., PA.

+ 28 F ii   Sarah Ann DEVOR.
+ 29 F iii   Carrie Ethel DEVOR.
30 M iv   Martin DEVOR, b. 14 Oct 1891, Spring Run, Franklin Co., PA; d. abe 1940. He was a sewing machine salesman. He was declared legally dead by California Court in 1940. He never married. (Carrie)

+ 31 F v   Juanita Alice DEVOR.
32 U vi   stillborn DEVOR, b. ca 1896.

Doras m.(2) Ada Mary NESBITT 26 May 1903, dau. of John Parshall NESBITT and Rhuemma SHEARER, b. 23 Jul 1878, Spring Run, Franklin Co., PA; d. 15 Jan 1947, Warren, Trumbull Co., OH; bur. Champion Cemetery, Champion, Trumbull Co., OH.

When Carrie DEVOR went to Montana in 1914, Doras DEVOR moved his family into Carrie's Spring Run home.

When Doras DEVOR died, Ada moved her children into the house of her father John Parshall NESBITT at Spring Run. Ada cared for her father and inherited her father's house upon his death. Anna GROSVENOR remembers the house as she visited Spring Run in 1923 and played in the creek by the DEVOR home.

Ada received one dollar yearly from the State of Pennsylvania as a widow. She sewed for people and made clothing for her children from clothing given to her. Her sister Etna NESBITT, Mrs. Rowland DAVIS and her husband helped by keeping the children with them in Barnsboro, PA during summers.

Ada's boys, Jesse and Walter, went to Warren, Ohio when they finished high school. Ada and Gladys joined them when Gladys graduated. Ada bought a bungalow on McMyler Street.

When Carrie's daughter Nora Grace HAWLEY contracted scarlet fever, Carrie's house was quarantined and Ada stayed with three of Carrie's children during the 30 day quarantine. Carrie stayed

with her sister Sarah and her baby daughter Betty so
that she could continue to go to work daily at the
Sunlight Electric Co.

Ada lived with the family of her daughter Gladys
GALPIN for several years prior to her death in 1947.
(Mary Devor) (Anna)

Children:
+   33 M vii   Walter Doras DEVOR.
+   34 M viii Jesse Eugene DEVOR.
+   35 F ix   Gladys Viola DEVOR.
    36 M x   Donald R. DEVOR, b. 2 Feb 1913, Spring Run,
               Franklin Co., PA; d. 11 Feb 1913, Spring
               Run, Franklin Co., PA.
               Donald died with jaundice and convulsions at
               9 days.

8   Anna Susan DEVOR, b. 21 May 1866, Spring Run, Franklin
    Co., PA; d. 13 Nov 1942, Spring Run, Franklin Co., PA;
    bur. Spring Run Cemetery, Franklin Co., PA.
       Anna taught school four terms before marriage.
    (Corwin)

    Anna m. (1) Arthur A. JOHNSTON 22 May 1889. Arthur,
    son of Samuel A. JOHNSTON and Margaret ADAMS, b. 7 May
    1866; d. 21 Jan 1947, Spring Run, Franklin Co., PA;
    bur. Spring Run Cemetery, Franklin Co., PA.
       Anna and Arthur were married by Thomas Dobbin.
    They spent their entire married life on the same farm
    and celebrated their Golden Anniversary May 22, 1938.
       Arthur JOHNSTON spent his younger days teaming,
    mostly in the woods, later took over the McCormick
    farm at Spring Run, PA. They lived in a stone house
    built in 1792, and in 1906 built a frame home.
    (Corwin)

Children:
+   37 M i   Jay Corwin JOHNSTON.
    38 M ii   Lester Wendell JOHNSTON, b. 27 Oct 1893,
              Spring Run, Franklin Co., PA; d. 18 Oct
              1918, Near Souilly, France; bur. Spring Run
              Cemetery, Franklin Co., PA.
                 Lester went overseas during World War
              I in Co. A. 304th M.P. He was a school
              teacher in Path Valley, PA before going
              overseas. He died at Souilly, France, just
              at the end of the First World War, from
              neglect during the Flu epidemic. His body
              was returned for burial at Spring Run, PA.
              (Corwin)

+   39 M iii   Samuel A. JOHNSTON.

9   Luetta May DEVOR, b. 9 May 1868, Spring Run, Franklin
    Co., PA; d. 26 Jan 1946, PA.

    Luetta m. (1) William Tecumseh STEELE 23 Dec 1895.
    William, b. 3 Aug 1869; d. 13 Mar 1939, PA.
        They lived their entire married life in
    Huntingdon Co., PA, farming.

Children:
    40 F i   Marie STEELE, b. 29 Oct 1896, Huntingdon,
               PA.
               Marie m. (1) Rev. Chalmers GOSHORN,
               Presbyterian minister in Maryland.

    41 M ii   Donald STEELE, b. 5 Oct 1898, Huntingdon,
               PA; d. 1970.
               Donald m. (1) Carrie LINN.
                   They lived in Harrisburg, PA. He
               worked on the railroad. Later he worked at
               an office job at Enola near Harrisburg, PA.

    42 F iii   Anna STEELE, b. 11 Jan 1902, Huntingdon, PA.
               Anna m. (1) Joseph "Joe" McILROY.
                   They lived in Huntingdon, PA. He was
               a realtor and salesman for automotive parts.

    43 M iv   Bruce STEELE, b. 23 Feb 1904, Huntingdon,
               PA; d. 26 Aug 1972.

               Bruce m. (1) Freda SHUE.
                   He was an engineer on the Pennsylvania
               Railroad and they lived at R.C. #3,
               Mechanicsburg, PA

                    THIRD GENERATION

12 Mary Lydica WALKER, b. 3 Nov 1875, Shirleysburg, PA;
    d. 10 Mar 1970; bur. 14 Mar 1970 German Valley
    Cemetery.

    Mary m. Newton NELSON 3 Mar 1897. Newton died 1914.

Children:
    44 F i   Hilda NELSON.
    45 F ii   Elizabeth NELSON.
    46 F iii   Mary NELSON.
+   47 F iv   Esther NELSON.

17 Zeola Belle WALKER, b. 11 Jun 1885, Shirley Twp.,
   Huntingdon Co., PA; d. 20 Jan 1962, Memorial Hospital,
   Bedford Co., PA; bur. 24 Jan 1962, Germany Valley,
   Stone Church Cemetery, Shirleysburg, Huntingdon Co.,
   PA.

   Zeola m. (1) Charles S. LIGHTNER 1923, Orbisonia, PA.
   Charles, son of John H. LIGHTNER and Mary Ellen
   BURKET, b. 21 Apr 1880, Shirleysburg, Huntingdon Co.,
   PA; d. 11 Sep 1965, Hospital, Altoona, Blair Co., PA;
   bur. 14 Sep 1965, Stone Church Cemetery, of The
   Brethern.
        They were married by Rev. McCowan.

Children:
+   48 F i   Jessie Cromwell LIGHTNER.

   Zeola m. (2) Ross CAMPBELL.

28 Sarah Ann DEVOR, b. 29 May 1887, Spring Run, Fannett
   Twp., Franklin Co., PA; d. 15 Sep 1953, Warren,
   Trumbull Co., OH; bur. Braceville Cemetery, Newton
   Falls, OH.

   Sarah m. (1) Solomon Warren "Sol" CROUSE 12 Sep 1912.
   by Rev. W.L. Murray of Spring Run United Brethern
   Church. "Sol" was a cousin of Sarah, the son of
   Solomon B. CROUSE and Margaret FRENCH.
        (Sarah and Sol were both great grandchildren of
        Jesse DEVOR.)

    49 U i   (_____) CROUSE. This child was born dead.

29 Carrie Ethel DEVOR, b. 1 Feb 1889, Spring Run,
   Franklin Co., PA; d. 19 Jul 1978, Yavapai Community
   Hospital, Prescott, Yavapai Co., AZ; bur. 20 Jul 1978,
   Rest Haven Cemetery, Glendale, Maricopa Co., AZ.
        Carrie attended school in Spring Run, PA and
   later Juniata College, working her way through. She
   taught two years of school in Pennsylvania and then
   went West to Malta, Montana, in 1914 to homestead land
   and teach school there.

   Carrie m. (1) Miller Henry HAWLEY 21 May 1916, Malta,
   Phillips Co., MT. Miller, son of Henry Allen HAWLEY
   and Rebecca Jane HALL, b. 19 Oct 1884, Christiansburg,
   Montgomery Co., VA; d. 21 June 1922, Malta, Phillips
   Co., MT; bur. Malta, Phillips Co., MT.
        Miller homesteaded 320 acres of land 12 miles
   southwest of Malta, Montana. He had consumption, now
   known as tuberculosis, which was the cause of his
   death at the young age of 37. (Anna)

Four children were born at the farm near Malta. Miller became ill with consumption and died on 21 June 1922. Carrie and the four small children rode a train to Warren, OH. Sister Sarah DEVOR CROUSE welcomed them and took the responsibility of bringing up baby Betty.

Carrie got a job at the Sunlight Electric Co. and worked long hours. Nora Grace developed tuberculosis of the spine apparently from having been held so much by her Daddy while Carrie was busy keeping house and taking care of the family.

Carrie, Anna and Ray lived in various rented places until 1924 when Carrie bought a house at 223 Vermont St.

Carrie hired someone to take care of the children in summer, except for the two times they spent six weeks at the Kiwanis Fresh Air Camp. In 1929 she moved the family to a larger house at 1533 McMyler St. This house had a real bathroom with a bath tub. This house was a little closer to her job, but she still had to walk two miles to work.

In 1935 Anna got a job at the Sunlight and that helped a lot. 1936 was a bad year as Nora Grace died at the TB Sanatorium at Howland and Anna was in the hospital for 3 months because of a burst appendix. In 1937 Ray started work at Republic Steel.

Carrie bought a Willys in 1937 but never learned to drive. Ray and Anna drove her on trips. One trip was made to see the homestead and old friends at Malta, MT. Another was to Callendar, Ont. via Niagara Falls to see the Dionne quintuplets. Betty was along on both trips. Carrie woke everyone to see a display of the Northern Lights when in Canada.

Carrie retired from the Sunlight and she with Ray and Anna purchased and divided an old unused 40 acre farm. Carrie got the house with four small rooms and no inside plumbing or electricity. She converted the house to a comfortable home with the help of Ray and Anna. Later when they married, Ray and Anna moved onto their respective parts of the farm.

By 1954, Ray, his wife Anna, and their three children were planning to move to Arizona for his health. Carrie sold her property and went with them to Phoenix, AZ. She bought a house within a block of theirs, but later had one built even closer to Ray's in the Sunnyslope area.

Over the years, Carrie gradually developed Alzheimer disease and in 1971 she spent about a year in a rest home. Anna retired from her job with the Prudential in 1972 and they moved to Camp Verde, AZ. She took her Mother there and cared for her until June 1978. Carrie appeared to enjoy the rural life with its chickens, geese and goats. In June 1978 she again entered a rest home, this time in Prescott, AZ. She died the 19th of July 1978. A memorial service was held for her in Camp Verde. (Anna)

+ 50 F i   Anna May Hawley
+ 51 M ii Ray Allen HAWLEY.
  52 F iii Nora Grace HAWLEY, b. 27 May 1920, Malta, Phillips Co., MT; Chr. 10 Sep 1922, United Brethern, Rev. M. P. Kindred, Malta, MT; d. 5 Jun 1936, County TB Hospital, Howland Twp., Trumbull Co., OH; bur. 8 Jun 1936, Crown Hill Cemetery, Howland Twp., Trumbull Co., OH.

When Nora Grace started to walk she didn't hold her head up as she should and was diagnosed as having tuberculosis of the spine. Her Daddy had held her a lot while her mother was caring for her little sister, Betty and all the rest of the household. She spent nearly two years on her back in a hospital bed in Youngstown, OH. Then another almost two years wearing a plaster body cast to hold her head up. This was changed periodically, until she was promoted to a brace which was worn like a corset around her middle with an iron rod up the back to support a chin piece. This was much better, for then she could take it off for sleeping and finally escape some of the confinement of all those years. She did finally graduate from the brace.

In the meantime, beginning when she was still wearing the cast, she was transported by members of the Rotary Club International to and from the Crippled Children's Class which was held at Central Junior High School. She was a good student and had a teacher she dearly loved, Miss Fuller.

For two summers Nora Grace, Ray and Anna were all invited to attend the Kiwanis Fresh Air Camp for six weeks and Nora Grace was there for a third year. She had many friends in both the Kiwanis and Rotary. She was privileged to ride in a parade in the car with "Gene and Glenn" of radio fame and take a meal with them at a hotel.

The 6th of Nov 1935 it was discovered that the old TB was breaking down and she would have to go to the TB San. She entered the Sanatorium about the first of December 1935.

She kept a diary beginning the 6th of
Nov. 1935, but didn't write in it every day.
Her last entry was 9 May 1936 and she died
5 June 1936.
Nora Grace wrote many poems in her
short life and the last and most memorable
one follows:
Oh, Mother, if you love me,
Don't let me die alone
Come put your arms around me
For I am going home.
I know you'll miss me sadly
But don't you worry dear,
For I will be so happy
With Jesus very near.
(Feb 1936, Age 15)

+   53 F iv   Betty Lois Hawley.

31 Juanita Alice DEVOR, b. 11 Dec 1893, Spring Run,
Franklin Co., PA; d. 31 Oct 1990, Warren, Trumbull
Co., OH; bur., Crown Hill Cemetery, Vienna, Trumbull
Co., OH.

Juanita m. (1) Frank Howard KALTENBAUGH 9 Sep 1922.
Frank, son of John KALTENBAUGH and Margaret Matilda
WEBER, b. 20 Mar 1890, PA; d. 9 Feb 1970, Warren,
Trumbull Co., OH; bur. Crown Hill Cemetery, Vienna
Twp., Trumbull Co.
Frank was a machinist at the Peerless Electric
Co. in Warren, OH and a W.W.I. Veteran. Upon
retirement he purchased a place in the country and
built a house he hoped to move into, but Juanita
refused to go. Frank made a garden on the new
property and visited it often.
Frank chewed tobacco for many years and died
because of the cancer which started in his mouth.
When Juanita and Frank were married they moved
into the house at 179 Oregon, Warren, OH and lived the
rest of their lives there. She died there at the age
97. The last I knew, her death date had not been put
on her stone in Crown Hill Cemetery.
After Frank died Juanita lived alone and as she
aged she did not take good care of herself or her
home. She dressed in ragged clothes and ate poorly.
She was a miser and kept $2,000 in the house. A
neighbor woman, Ronnie Dever came to visit her and
helped with the housework.
One night Juanita was robbed by a young man who
had worked for her. He knocked her down and jammed
the door against her so that she could not move. She

was found two days later and taken to the home of Bruce KALTENBAUGH, a grandson.

After several months she recovered and moved back into her home. At this time Ronnie Dever had a fight with her husband and moved into Juanita's house. Ronnie took care of Juanita until her death. She did all the shopping and housework and when Juanita became bed ridden, Ronnie brought her meals up to the second floor bedroom. She paid Juanita's bills and prepaid an expensive funeral for her. Ronnie received her room and board, but got no salary. Upon Juanita's death Ronnie received the house.

Children:
+ 54 M i   Allen KALTENBAUGH.

33 Walter Doras DEVOR b. 18 Aug 1906, Spring Run, Franklin Co., PA; d. 16 May 1992, St. Elizabeth Hosp. Youngstown, Mahoning Co., OH; bur. 20 May 1992, Hubbard Union Cemetery, Hubbard, Trumbull Co., OH.

Walter was 8 years old when his father died. His mother, Ada, moved the family into the home of their grandfather, John Parshall NESBITT, and kept house for her father and children.

Walter was sickly as a child and had pneumonia more than once. Even so, he was farmed out to a local farmer for his room and board and ten cents a day. His brother Jesse caught up with him in school and when they graduated they went to Warren, Ohio, where they had three half sisters from their father's first wife. His mother and younger sister Gladys joined them when Gladys graduated from high school

Walter Doras DEVOR m. (1) Dorothy T. GORDON 8 Jul 1929. Dorothy, b. 18 Oct 1909; d. 29 Jun 1986, Hubbard, Trumbull Co., OH.

Dorothy was a grade school teacher for many years. She taught at Hubbard, Ohio and attended the Presbyterian church. In 1986 Walter was away on a job for a few days and when he came home he found her dead on the floor by the living room couch.

Walter and Dorothy lived in Hubbard, OH at 156 Hager St. for many years. In 1984 he retired from the Lombard Corporation of Youngstown, Ohio, where he had worked for 21 years as a design engineer. They were manufacturers of machinery and Walter did many other jobs at different times over the years. Late in his life he was bothered by arthritis.

He died of congestive heart failure.

Children:
+ 55 M i   Ronald W. DEVOR.
+ 56 M ii   Michael G. DEVOR.

34 Jesse Eugene DEVOR, b. 30 Dec 1907, Spring Run, Franklin Co., PA; d. 2 Mar 1977, McAllen, TX; bur. Crown Hill Cemetery, Vienna Twp., Trumbull Co., OH.

Jesse was seven years old when his father died. His widowed mother did sewing for income. Jesse worked for local farmers and received room, board and ten cents a day. In the early 1920's he went to Warren, OH, where his half sisters were living and got a job at General Fireproofing. When his sister Gladys graduated from high school Ada brought the rest of her family to Warren.

Jesse married Ruth CRYTZER and they had a daughter, Sally (WHITE). The marriage ended when Ruth took off with the mail carrier. Jesse paid child support until Sally was 16.

Jesse m. (1) Mary Ann TAKACH. Mary dau. of Joseph "Joe" TAKACH and Katalina FEDELEM, b. 4 Mar 1914, Hungary, d. 5 Aug 1998 at nursing home. Her body to go to Northeastern College of medicine and internment at Crown Hill Cemetery, Howland, Trumbull Co., OH.

In 1921 Mary and her mother came to the U.S. and went to Girard, Ohio, to join her father who had come to the U.S. and obtained a job with the A.M. Byers Company of Girard, Ohio. Her father was tall and strong. His job was to push a wheelbarrow load of slag and dump it in the blast furnace. When Mary arrived in Girard they lived in a four room house with no bathroom, electricity or ice box.

Mary walked a mile to a Catholic school. She spoke no English at first and no one in the school spoke Hungarian. However, she learned English and in 1933 graduated from Cortland High School. In 1927 the A.M. Byers Company moved to Pennsylvania and Joseph TAKACH bought a farm at Nutwood, Ohio. He farmed with horses at first and later bought a tractor. Mary learned to care for pigs and chickens, raise vegetables and milk cows.

Mary met Jesse DEVOR at a dance hall at Cortland during her senior year. Jesse came to her graduation to hear her talk. She graduated with honors. Mary soon had a piece work job at the Sunlight Electric Co. They were married in Wellsburg, West Virginia in July 1933. They lived in an apartment on Tod Avenue in Warren for a year and then moved to Southington.

He was laid off soon after his marriage but obtained a job with Republic Steel. Jesse pitched for the Company baseball team and later played second base. The labor union went on strike in 1935. Jesse needed the job and found that he could get through the picket lines by crawling through a sewer pipe. The union won the strike. When the steel business became bad Jesse was laid off and worked as a group leader on WPA, but he was soon called back to Republic Steel.

Mary wrote, "Somewhere earlier Jesse married a Ruth CRYTZER and had a daughter Sally. Ruth took off with her mail carrier, a Mr. WHITE, who left his wife and daughter also. I did meet his wife a couple times. Jesse supported Sally through Youngstown Courts, no visiting privileges. When Ruth found out Jesse and I were married she told a bunch of lies in court to Humane Society and Jesse just kept quiet but I said 'I'm going down and tell the Humane Society the truth to protect my twin babies in 1934-5 that Jesse was no bum, etc. So Ruth had her husband adopt Sally. Jesse and I always thought Sally (DEVOR WHITE) would hunt us up sometime after her mother Ruth died for Jesse was not what she was taught. Through Dorothy (Walter's wife) just before Dorothy died, Sally inquired for a picture of Jesse. Her dad and I were willing but contacts were lost. So not knowing, Sally's married name or whereabouts is also lost. Yes, I've seen Ruth, never spoke to her directly. Also saw Sally before, when she was a child, on 2 occasions--court order with Jesse." (Mary TAKACH DEVOR)

When World War II started, Jesse left Republic Steel to work for American Welding where he could earn overtime pay and help the war effort. Jesse and Mary were living at Southington in a tiny house on two unimproved acres where their children Gladys and Tom were born. Mary also worked at a factory job. They added rooms and a basement to this house and acreage to their farm. They built a barn and a lake for a place for Jesse to fish.

Mary worked in the factory during the early years of their marriage. She gave this up to care for her large garden and her widowed mother. She and Jesse went to Spring Run each year for the Path Valley Picnic and Mary became acquainted with many of Jesse's relatives. Mary had a hobby of collecting cow shaped cream pitchers. At one time she had 400.

Jesse also did plumbing in the evenings in addition to his job. He studied and became a Master Plumber. Often Mary helped on his plumbing jobs. For recreation Jess and Mary hunted pheasants, fished and went to the annual Path Valley Reunions in Spring Run.

In 1947 Jesse left American Welding to work at Standard Steel Spring of Newton Falls, OH. He hammered out the first bumper and started a career that lasted 23 years. When the General Foreman left, Jesse was promoted to his job. This job was wearing as he had to work seven days a week, if needed, but

Jesse liked the job. He was diagnosed with diabetes in 1955 and the job got harder.

In 1970 Jess retired and he and Mary started spending their winters in McAllen, Texas. The climate there was moderate and the fishing good. He died the second of March 1977 on the way home from a day of enjoyable fishing. (Mary)

After Jesse's death, Mary lived in an apartment in Warren and visited daughter Gladys in Maple Heights, Ohio and son Tom in Austin, Texas. After Tom's death she was ill and Gladys moved her to Maple Heights to her home. There she met Owen DICKINSON and they married and lived near Gladys.

Children:
57 F i   Gladys Ada (twin) DEVOR, b. 14 Dec 1934, Warren Trumbull Co., OH.

Gladys is an avid baseball fan. She attended Asbury College in Kentucky. Two of the teachers there were John Wesley DEVOR and his wife Blanche. Gladys taught grade school at Maple Heights, Ohio for many years and retired there.

58 F ii   Alyce Kay (twin) DEVOR, b. 14 Dec 1934, Trumbull Co., OH: d. Dec 1934, Trumbull Co., OH; bur. Crown Hill Cemetery, Vienna Twp., Trumbull Co., OH.

59 M iii Thomas DEVOR, b. 15 Sep 1936, Warren, Trumbull Co., OH: d. 1991, Austin, TX; bur. Crown Hill Cemetery, Howland, Trumbull Co., OH.

Tom, a Chalker High School graduate, received his Bachelor of Arts degree from Asbury College and took extra courses at Western Reserve, Cleveland; University of Alaska, Fairbanks; and Southern Illinois University, Carbondale, IL. He completed six years of teaching in Alaska at Eielson Air Base High School.

He also spent time in Vietnam during the Vietnam War. He retired and lived in Austin, Texas. He never did marry although it was reported at one time that he was planning to get married. (Anna)

He attended Texas Tech. College under a National Science Foundation grant. While there he also went to Taos, New Mexico, for field trips. Later he went to Tripoli, Libya, to teach biology at Whellus Air Base High School.

While at Eielson High School he was on a committee for State of Alaska Department of Education Aerospace Science Education Curriculum Committee. Devor wrote the first syllabus for State of Alaska on the aerospace program.

The year book "Raven" of the Eielson High School was dedicated to Devor in 1965. This same year he earned the coveted "Teacher of the Year" award.

While in Alaska he taught lab-science and aerospace in 1965-66.

35 Gladys Viola DEVOR, b. 20 Feb 1910, Spring Run, Franklin Co., PA; d. 28 Jul 1983, Warren, Trumbull Co., OH; bur. 30 Jul 1983, Champion Cemetery, Champion, Trumbull Co., OH.

Gladys m. (1) Eugene Charles "Gene" GALPIN, Eugene, b. 12 Mar 1903; d. 23 Dec 1994, Trumbull Memorial Hospital, Warren, Trumbull Co., OH; bur. 27 Dec 1994, Crown Hill Burial Park, Vienna, Trumbull Co., OH.

Gene and Gladys met where they both worked at the Sunlight Electric Plant in Warren, Ohio. The company policy at the time was that husband and wife would not be employed. So they married secretly, but when pregnancy hit they had to reveal the marriage. They lived at 1635 State Rd. NW, Warren, OH.

Gladys suffered from multiple sclerosis and diabetes. In a letter of 20 Dec 1971 she stated that she had more things wrong with her than MS but it was quite boring. She was buried July 30, 1983 at Champion Cemetery beside her mother, Ada Nesbitt Devor. Gene died of congestive heart failure at age 91.

Children:
+ 60 F i   Devor Jean GALPIN.

37 Jay Corwin JOHNSTON, b. 23 Mar 1890, Spring Run, Franklin, OH; d. 14 Oct 1965; bur. Spring Run Cemetery, Spring Run, PA.

Corwin m. (1) Sadie REED 25 Jun 1911. Sadie, b. 4 Oct 1887, Toledo, OH; d. 26 Nov 1969.

Sadie was a classmate of Corwin Johnston at Ohio Northern University. She taught in the Allenport schools and was active in the Presbyterian Church.

Corwin studied electrical engineering and graduated from Ohio Northern University. He took education courses at Penn State University. After college he worked for six years as an engineer at Willys Overland of Toledo, Ohio. He then farmed in Spring Run until 1926 when he moved to Mt. Union, PA where he taught mathematics and industrial arts for 27 years.

He worked as an apiary specialist for the Department of Agriculture, and in summers toured every state in the Union, Canada, and Mexico. He was active in the Boy Scouts and served as a troop committeeman and as a district officer. He served as a trustee and treasurer in the First Presbyterian Church of Mount Union and held the position of Sunday School Superintendent for five years.

In 1960 when Jesse Devor asked for some genealogical information, Corwin sent it to him and told him if he wanted more to come to see him as he had loads of it which he had raked from court records, cemeteries, church records, state library, etc. for the past 30 years.

Corwin and Sadie celebrated their 50th Wedding Anniversary on 25 June 1961.

Children:
    61 M i   Robert JOHNSTON, b. 3 Jun 1912.
                Robert lives at Coatesville, PA and operates a diesel on the Reading R.R. He and his wife Mary have a daughter Pearl Louise. (Corwin)

39 Samuel A. JOHNSTON m. (1) Miss (_____).
    Sam's wife died after 8 years as an invalid.

Children:
    62 F i   Edith Catharine "Edie Kay" JOHNSTON, b. ca 1918. Edie Kay is an only daughter. She is married and has two children. (1983)

47 Esther NELSON m. (1) Gene SHERRER. Gene, d. 25 Dec 1977.

Children:
    63 M i   Robert SHERRER, b. Feb 1948.
    64 F ii   Barbara SHERRER, b. ca 1952.
                In college she majored in Home Economics with a minor in Biology. She graduated in June 1973 and started teaching at Austintown.

49 Jessie Cromwell LIGHTNER, b. 15 May 1924, Shirleysburg, Huntingdon Co., PA.

Jessie m. Harry Grant CALHOUN 3 Dec 1960, Harry, b. 10

May 1928, 29 E. 4th Ave., Everett, W. Providence Twp., Bedford Co., PA.

After marriage they took up housekeeping at W. 6th Ave., R.D. #3, Everett, PA.

Children:
- 65 F i   Deborah May "Debbie" CALHOUN, b. 29 May 1962, Snake Spring Twp., PA; d. 13 Aug 1966, Everett, W. Providence Twp., Bedford Co., PA; bur. Everett Cemetery, W. Providence Twp., Bedford Co., PA.
- 66 M ii   Gregory Grant "Greg" CALHOUN, b. 19 Apr 1964, Bedford Memorial Hospital, Snake Spring Twp, Bedford Co., PA.

50 Anna May HAWLEY, b. 21 Feb 1917, Malta, Phillips Co., MT; chr. 10 Sep 1922, United Brethern, Malta, Phillips Co., MT. At the age of 18 she was bedridden for about six months as the result of a burst appendix. Many prayers and a fine nurse were her healing blessing.

Anna m. (1) Richard "Dick" Browne GROSVENOR Thursday, the 13th May 1943, Warren, Trumbull Co., OH. Richard, son of Fred Browne GROSVENOR, M.D. and Olive Evangeline SWICKARD, b. 29 Apr 1916, Columbus, Franklin Co., OH.

Dick graduated from college and was a high school history teacher. He spent 13 months in the Army, training in Mississippi. When his father died the Army released him to be bread winner for his mother.

Dick and Anna met at a dance. Anna had been working at the Sunlight for eight years and quit that job in anticipation of becoming a housewife.

Dick worked at defense work during W.W.II. Anna worked for a short time at the Lordstown Ordinance Depot driving a lift.

Dick and Anna first lived in Newton Falls, OH. It was wartime and many things besides meat and sugar were being rationed. Anna owned a 26 acre plot of land on the Center of the World South Rd. west of Leavittsburg, OH. They wanted to build a house, but the rules were: "No new houses" because of rationing. They ordered a prefabricated farm building from Sears, and installed a concrete block foundation. The building came in large sections to be bolted together. The front wall had four sets of windows. The roof was a big curve which curved down to the ground at the rear. They made it livable with some plumbing, electricity, insulation and furniture.

When the war was over. They had help building a big double garage. Dick was working as a Jewel Tea Co. Salesman. He sold groceries and housewares on a rural sales route. He used the garage to keep the weekly stock for his route of customers.

Both daughters were born while they lived there. About 1951 they bought a real house on Kale-Adams Road about a half mile from the first house. It also had a garage for the Jewel Tea Co. stock. The house had a cellar, and a big porch on two sides.

In 1953 Dick decided to go back to Kent State University for his Masters Degree. He got a job at the Kent Twin Coach Co. working on the 3 to 11 shift. He roomed in Kent and attended school from 9 to 2. After eight months of school they sold the house on Kale-Adams Rd. and bought a 41 foot house trailer and lived at the Klesa Trailer Park at Stow. Dick continued at school but had severe eye trouble. He was unable to finish his schooling and in April 1955 the Grosvenor family went to Arizona. That trip could use a lot of space in a story, but they made it!

Anna's mother and brother Ray and his family had gone to Arizona the year before. Anna and Dick parked their house trailer for awhile on the acre of land that Ray owned in Phoenix. Dick tried to find a job but was not having any luck and he wanted to move on to San Diego. So Anna decided to go job hunting. She came home that night with a temporary job in the office of the Registrar of Contractors. It was the time of year that contractors had to renew their licenses. She did well, the job lasted about 4 years until an election put her boss out of work.

During that time they saw an ad of someone who wanted to trade their house for a travel trailer. The house was on Harmont Drive in Sunnyslope and the trade was made.

At Phoenix Dick worked for the Phoenix Indian Hospital for six years. This job was only half paper work at first but as the years went on the paper work increased and the physical stock work became less. He left the job and returned to school teaching.

During their time in Arizona they spent many weekends exploring all the parks and places of interest and took many slide pictures of that beautiful state.

There were some very nice lakes in the area and Anna wanted to find out how a sail boat works, so they bought a small styrofoam sail boat. It had a dagger board instead of a keel. They spent some weekends camping and sailing.

When she lost her job, Anna went to a private school for awhile to brush up on her shorthand and typing. Then she luckily got a secretarial job at The Prudential Insurance Co., Mortgage Loan Office. She was there for 12 years and retired.

When she retired they had a house built and moved to an acre lot at Camp Verde, AZ. Dick then taught school at Cottonwood, a 20 mile drive from Camp Verde. They made garden and had chickens, geese, goats and raised a calf.

Anna'a mother enjoyed being there on their little farm with the chickens, etc. When she became so ill that Anna couldn't take care of her any longer, she was moved to a nursing home in Prescott and only lived about a month longer.

They moved to Vida, OR in 1978 where she does volunteer work. She schedules patrol runs for the Vida-McKenzie Neighborhood Watch. As a result of this scheduling she has been promoting a 13 month calendar to start with the Year 2000. Each month would have 28 days, start on Sunday and end on Saturday, which would help a lot to keep track of dates. Each year would start the New Year with a very special holiday with no number that would be called NEW YEAR DAY. When leap year comes around, it would also be an extra holiday also unnumbered at the end of the year and be named LEAP YEAR DAY.

Anna volunteers at the Oregon Genealogical Society, preparing the member's Pedigrees for publication and working two days a month at the library repairing books. She records the finances of the McKenzie Valley Presbyterian Church on her computer. She is a member and an officer of the Grange.

Dick follows his hobbies of bird watching, walking, swimming and genealogy. He has written "The Ancestry and Descendants of John Grosvenor of Roxbury, MA." published in 1997 by Heritage Books, Inc.

Children:
+ 67 F i   Dorothy Jean GROSVENOR.
   68 F ii   Susan Mae GROSVENOR, b. 19 Apr 1950, Warren, Trumbull Co., OH.

Born in Ohio, Susan grew up in the Arizona desert where the family enjoyed camping and exploring Indian ruins. She studied piano from the age of seven and later violin, cello and other instruments. She graduated 5th in her high school class and won second place in the Phoenix Symphony Guild Concerto Competition. She received scholarships to the San Francisco Conservatory of Music and to Arizona State University where she majored in music.

Susan m. (1) James "Jim" Findley KENNEDY, Jr. 12 Dec 1971, Phoenix, Maricopa Co., AZ; they divorced. James, b. 5 Nov 1949.

She and Jim hitchhiked from Arizona to New Hampshire and back before starting their first music group. For years, they played in music groups throughout the western states.

In the 1980's Susan settled down to the work of teaching music and composing music for short films, videos, theater and radio. After releasing an album of piano compositions she guested on a CD of various artists.

She found that when she focused her attention on people she would hear music and practiced a method of music therapy whereby she would translate the sounds she heard from an individual into recorded music. The music was known to bring people into deepened states of relaxed awareness and trigger healing.

Susan m. (2) Paul Douglas SPEARS 24 Dec 1989, Portland, OR. Paul, son of Douglas Duane SPEERS and Alice CHAPMAN, b. 11 Jan 1965, Seattle, King Co., WA.

Paul majored in geography and received his B.S. degree from the U. of Oregon in 1989. He once composed sound tracks for the shows at the planetarium at Eugene, OR.

Susan met Paul Spears when he studied piano with her. They married in a private ceremony on Christmas Eve 1989. They had a public ceremony the following summer on the banks of the McKenzie River in Leaburg, OR near the home of her parents. They moved to Arizona where Paul works at the Arizona Sonora Desert Museum. Susan plays organ at a local church and continues her music work.

51 Ray Allen HAWLEY, b. 5 Nov 1918, Malta, Phillips Co., MT; d. 22 Feb 1980, Golden, Jefferson Co., CO; bur. Golden, Jefferson Co., Colorado. He was cremated.

Ray was a good student in school. He wanted to write with his left hand but his teacher made him learn to use his right hand. He was the smallest boy in his class in grade school but grew up to be normal.

Ray m. Anna Frances WEIR 24 Aug 1940, Warren, Trumbull Co., OH, Anna, dau. of James Summerville WEIR and Leah Amelia BIEBER, b. 11 Feb 1921, Odessa, FL.

As a child Anna lived at 905 Palmyra Rd., Warren OH. Their wedding was solemnized at the bride's home by Rev. George W. Peters of Tod Ave. Methodist Church.

She wore her mother's wedding gown of white embroidered lawn. Anna was graduated from Harding H.S. in Jan 1939 and both were employed at the Sunlight Electric Division of General Motors Corp.

As a bride she and Ray moved to his property at Leavittsburg, OH. Ray got work as a machinist at Republic Steel in Niles, OH and they lived at Warren and then Leavittsburg. He became afflicted with Multiple Sclerosis at the age of 27. It was then in 1954 they moved to Phoenix, AZ because of Ray's health, taking their family of 3 children with them. Anna worked in a General Electric Company factory and later in a Health Food Store. When she retired they moved to Golden, CO to the house of Jim, their oldest son. They attended a Baptist church for many years and Anna played catcher on the the young people's baseball team.

Children:
69 M i   James Henry HAWLEY, b. 12 Jan 1942, Warren, Trumbull Co., OH.

Jim was a member of the Marines for a time. He worked for the telephone company, both in Phoenix, AZ and Denver, CO and took early retirement.

James m. (1) Sandra Kay PRICE 29 Aug 1964. Sandra, dau. of Kenneth Marion PRICE and Helen Gail AMES, b. 11 Jul 1943, Kansas City, Jackson Co., MO.

She is a retired Savings & Loan Co. employee. She enjoys genealogy, her computer and the internet. She has a collection of several hundred cook books.

Jim likes to bowl and play golf. He and Sandy travel to national bowling tournaments and at times win money.

+ 70 F ii   Janice Eileen HAWLEY.
+ 71 M iii Robert Ray HAWLEY.

53 Betty Lois HAWLEY, b. 26 Oct 1921, Malta, Phillips Co., MT; chr. 10 Sep 1922, United Brethern, Rev. M. P. Kindred, Malta, MT; d. 26 Aug 1945, Warren City Hospital, Warren, Trumbull Co., OH; bur. 28 Aug 1945, Crown Hill Cemetery, Howland, Trumbull Co., OH.

Betty was a secretary at Copperweld Steel Co., and a Homemaker. Betty lived with her Aunt Sarah and Uncle Sol Crouse from the time she was about one year old until she married. She became an accomplished pianist.

Betty m. (1) Frank Edward CARBAUGH 23 Feb 1943, Warren, Trumbull Co., OH. Frank, son of Frank CARBAUGH and Sarah HOOD, b. 15 Jan 1921, Mt. Pleasant, Westmoreland Co., PA; d. 2 Jan 1993, Trumbull Memorial Hospital, Trumbull Co., OH; bur. Crown Hill Burial Park, Trumbull Co., OH

Frank was a 1939 graduate of Warren G. Harding High School and had attended Youngstown State University. He was a past exalted ruler of the Warren Elks Lodge No. 295. At the time of their marriage he was employed at Copperweld Steel Co. Betty and Frank were married by Rev. G. W. Peters in Tod Ave Methodist Church, Warren, OH. Both were graduates of Warren G. Harding H. S. Later Frank was a project engineer for Wean United.

Children:
+ 72 M i   David Frank CARBAUGH.

Frank m. (2) Pauline Studer, Apr 1, 1950.

Children:
James SINNHUBER (Pauline had married before and Jim was her son.)

72+M ii   Daniel CARBAUGH (Their son)

54 Allen KALTENBAUGH, b. 9 Jun 1923, Warren, Trumbull Co., OH; d. 4 Nov 1963, Warren, Trumbull Co., OH.

Allen m. (1) Lucille GREGGS 18 Sep 1942, Warren, Trumbull Co., OH. Lucille, b. 21 Feb 1924.
Allen worked as a machinist at the Peerless Electric in Warren and served in World War II. He died in his sleep of a heart attack. (Anna)

+ 73 M i   Bruce Allen KALTENBAUGH.
+ 74 M ii   Leslie Dean KALTENBAUGH.

55 Ronald W. DEVOR, b. 26 Aug 1940, Hubbard, Trumbull Co., OH. Lives at La Habra, CA.

Ronald m. (1) Vicki (_____). Vicki, b. 1 Apr 1938.

Children:
75 F i   Francy DEVOR, b. 27 Sep 1967.
76 F ii   Kathy DEVOR, b. 15 Apr 1960.

56 Michael G. DEVOR, b. 23 Jan 1948, Hubbard, Trumbull, Co., OH.

Michael m. (1) Ruth JAMESON. Ruth, b. 23 Jan 1948.

Children:
       77 F i   Kelly Kristine DEVOR, b. 22 Aug 1976.
       78 F ii   Erica DEVOR, b. 1978.

60 Devor Jean GALPIN, b. 6 Feb 1941, Warren, Trumbull
   Co., OH; chr. 27 Jul 1941, Presbyterian Church,
   Champion, Trumbull Co., OH.
       Devor graduated from Champion H. S. in May 1959.

   Devor m. (1) Richard "Dick" L. TAYLOR. Richard, son
   of William Barclay TAYLOR, Sr. and Alice Irene
   BEIGHLEY, b. 24 Feb 1936. His wedding attendants were
   William Taylor as Best Man, with Robert Taylor and
   Charles Taylor as ushers.
       Devor's Maid of Honor was Gladys DEVOR. Her
   bridesmaids were Sara Jane Taylor and Mrs. William
   Taylor, Jr.
       Devor and Dick live at Warren, Ohio. He services
   vending machines.

Children;
       79 F i   Violet Ann TAYLOR, b. 30 Jun 1975. She was
                 an Honor student when in the fifth Grade and
                 is learning to play the clarinet. Has had
                 problems with her right foot.

       80 F ii   Robin Irene TAYLOR, b. 8 Aug 1977. Robin is
                 studying guitar.

                      FIFTH GENERATION

67 Dorothy Jean GROSVENOR, b. 18 Jul 1945, Warren,
   Trumbull Co., OH.
       Dorothy graduated in 1963 with honors in
   secretarial courses and journalism from Sunnyslope
   High School in Phoenix, AZ. She immediately began a
   career in the legal field, first as a legal secretary
   and later as a paralegal. She was a member of and
   pursued her continuing education through Pacific
   Northwest Legal Assistants.

   Dorothy m. (1) Jack Lee WILLIAMS 18 Jul 1963, Phoenix,
   Maricopa Co., AZ; they divorced. Jack, son of Alfred
   WILLIAMS, twin, and Edna Lee CANEER, b. 23 Nov 1940,
   E. St. Louis, IL.
       Jack was a Health Spa worker. After his divorce
   from Dorothy he left Phoenix and did not return. His
   address is unknown.

Children:
+ 81 F i   Renee Yvonne WILLIAMS

Dorothy m. (2) Stanley Loren HALL 25 Aug 1972; they divorced.   Loren, son of David HALL and Dorothy (_____), b. 6 Mar 1944, Phoenix, AZ
     Loren was a truck driver during his marriage to Dorothy.

Dorothy m. (3) Norman D. CHOLEWINSKI 30 Aug 1988, Eugene, Lane Co., OR.   Norman, son of Edward CHOLEWINSKI and Hazel May RUCKER, b. 6 Mar 1956 at Fairbanks, AL.
     Norman obtained his B.S.E.E. from Oregon State U. in 1981. From 1988 to 1997 he was a sole proprietor consulting in the areas of instrumentation and rehabilitation engineering under the name of Performance Data Systems. In 1997 he joined another company.
     Other interests include photography, running, music and international travel. He and Dorothy are restoring their country property in Springfield, OR.
     After 30 years in law, Dorothy left to pursue other interests, including a longtime love of travel and gardening. She studied French and business at Lane Community College in Eugene, OR. She and Norm travel often in Europe and taught a class at the local Community College on travel in France.

70 Janice Eileen HAWLEY, b. 27 May 1943, Warren, Trumbull Co., OH.

Janice m. (1) The Rev. Harold Ward "Bud" HAMBLEY 3 Nov 1961, Phoenix, Maricopa Co., AZ. Bud, son of Lester A. HAMBLEY and Lucy I. THIESSEN, b. ca 1940, Elyria, Lorain Co., OH.
     Bud celebrates his birthday 20 Dec. He is a Baptist minister, and graduated from Golden Gate Baptist Theological Seminary, 31 May 1972. Received degree of Doctor of Philosophy from California Graduate School of Theology, 25 May 1979. In the fall of 1987 he published the book "JOSHUA, A MODEL FOR LEADERSHIP".

Children:
+ 82 F i   Kathryn Eileen "Kathy" HAMBLEY.
+ 83 F ii   Kimberly Ann "Kim" HAMBLEY.
+ 84 F iii   Kristina "Tina" Lynn HAMBLEY.
+ 85 F iv   Gloria Kay HAMBLEY.
 + 86 M v   Alan Ward HAMBLEY.

71   Robert Ray HAWLEY, b. 21 May 1946, Warren, Trumbull
Co., OH. Bob attended college and received a degree
in engineering. Has worked for the public utilities
company in Denver.

Robert m. (1) Connie DESKINS 7 Jun 1968, Phoenix,
Maricopa Co., AZ; they divorced. Connie, dau. of
Minor Harvey DESKINS and Aletha Jane CROY, b. 23 May
1949.

Children:
87 F i   Karlyn Kay HAWLEY, b. 27 Oct 1969. Karlyn
          works two jobs. She and Brian are living
          together. Brian (_____) is the father of an
          8 year old girl. (Anna Hawley letter, 26
          Jan 1995.)

88 F ii   Stephanie Arlene HAWLEY, b. 25 Apr 1971.
          Stephanie and Charles (_____) bought a home
          together.

89 M iii Robert Richard "Robbie" HAWLEY b. 23 Nov
          1973.

          Robert m. (1) Jenn (_____) 21 Nov 1994.
          Jenn has a boy, Mikel (_____).

Robert Ray m. (2) Elizabeth (REFFLE) HOUSEMAN 14 Feb
1982, NV. Elizabeth dau. of Josef REFFLE and Barbara
THOMAS, b. 15 Oct 1947, Craig Co., VA.
     Bob and Elizabeth were married about 1:00 at
Candle Light Chapel, after waiting almost 2 hours.
Elizabeth's sister flew in from California for the
wedding. (Anna Hawley)

72   David Frank CARBAUGH, b. 26 Aug 1945, Warren,
Trumbull Co., OH.
     David teaches Spanish at Warren G. Harding H. S.
in Warren, Ohio. While still in high school he spent
part of one summer in Mexico and visited the Grosvenor
family in Phoenix, Arizona, on his way home. He has
a hobby of visiting Indian Reservations and collecting
Indian stories and artifacts. (Anna)

David m. (1) Jeri Lynn MILLER 5 Jul 1969, St.
William's Church, Euclid, OH. Jeri, b. 16 May 1946.
     Jeri teaches Beginning Spanish at Warren G.
Harding H. S. in Warren, OH.

Children:
90 F i   Laurie Ann CARBAUGH, b. 15 Apr 1972, Warren,
          Trumbull Co., OH

Laurie is a student at Youngstown College and works part time in 1995.

91 M ii   Brian Allen CARBAUGH, b. 23 Jul 1974, Warren, Trumbull Co., OH.
Brian graduated from Hiram College in 1996 and won a scholarship to the law school of the University of Dayton.

73   Bruce Allen KALTENBAUGH, b. 1 Jan 1944.

Bruce m. (1) Darlene HOLANDBAUGH 2 Sep 1966. Darlene, b. 10 Aug 1946.

Children:
    92 F i   Gayle KALTENBAUGH, b. 10 Jul 1967.
    93 F ii   Jill KALTENBAUGH, b. 30 Jun 1970.

74   Leslie Dean KALTENBAUGH, b. 21 Oct 1946, Warren, Trumbull Co., OH.

Leslie m. (1) Tery TANERI 18 Sep 1965; they divorced.

Children:
    94 F i   Tracy KALTENBAUGH, b. 26 Aug 1966.
    95 F ii   Stacy KALTENBAUGH, b. 11 Jan 1969.

SIXTH GENERATION

81   Renee Yvonne WILLIAMS, b. 6 May 1964, Phoenix, Maricopa Co., AZ; chr. Jan 1965, Cross Roads Methodist Church Phoenix, Maricopa Co., AZ.
    Renee attended Marist High School in Eugene, OR and earned an A.A. at Lane Community College. She briefly attended the University of Oregon and continued her education at Lane Community College, becoming a licensed massage therapist. She pursues international travel and photography.

Renee m. (1) Craig Randall SORSETH 9 Apr 1994, Sweet Home, Linn Co., OR.

Craig, son of Alvin Lloyd "Tyke" SORSETH and Arlene Joyce SPORTSMAN, b. 6 May 1947, Sweet Home, Linn Co., OR
    Craig earned a B.S. in political science and an M.S. in Public Administration at the University of Oregon and works for the State of Oregon. He and Renee, with their son Noah, lived on the property homesteaded by his grandparents in Sweet Home, OR.

Children:
    96 M i   Noah Nakai SORSETH, b. 12 Aug 1996, Sweet
                Home, Linn Co., OR.

82 Kathryn Eileen "Kathy" HAMBLEY, b. 20 Dec 1962,
   Phoenix, Maricopa Co., AZ.
        Kathy graduated from Ocean View High School,
   Huntingdon Beach, CA., Jun 10, 1981.

   Kathy m. (1) Werner G. "Vern" HENSCHEL 29 Jul 1989,
   First Baptist Church, Banning, CA.
        They lived in Banning, CA in 1995. He works at
   Apple and does extra jobs on his own. Kathy teaches
   high school.

    97 M i   Brandon Kai HENSCHEL, 31 Jan 1991.

83 Kimberly Ann "Kim" HAMBLEY, b. 25 Feb 1964, Phoenix,
   Maricopa Co., AZ.
        Kim graduated from Ocean View High School in June
   1982.

   Kimberly m. Wesley "Wes" JOHNSON 18 Aug 1984,
   Westminster, Los Angeles, CA. Wesley, son of Gene
   JOHNSON.

Children:
    98 M i   Daniel Scott JOHNSON, b. 11 Jun 1987.
                "Just what we've been waiting for...
                a new little baby to love and adore."

    99 F ii   Cristen JOHNSON, b. May 1990.

    100M iii   Brandon JOHNSON, b. 31 Jan 1991.

84 Kristina "Tina" Lynn HAMBLEY, b. 12 Mar 1966.
        Tina graduated from Nursing School, and passed
   her state board, and became engaged to Marc.

   Kristina m. Marc Jeffrey VENABLE 4 Mar 1995 at The
   Dream Maker, Chapel #1, Incline Village, NV. Marc has
   a son. They moved to Arkansas.

85 Gloria Kay HAMBLEY, b. 29 Feb 1968. Graduated from
   Ocean View High School, Huntingdon Beach, CA., 18 Jun
   1986. Worked in Graphic Arts in 1995.

   Gloria Kay HAMBLEY m. Richard Eugene HALL 3 Sep 1994,
   Richard, son of Mr and Mrs. Orin HALL.

86 Alan Ward HAMBLEY, b. 19 Aug 1971.

Alan m. Jodi MITCHELL at 1st Southern Baptist Church in Lakewood, CA, 13 Jul 1991.

Children:
    101F i   Brooke Ariel HAMBLEY, b. 29 Jan 1992.
    102F ii   Katelynn Marie HAMBLEY, b. 12 Oct 1993

DESCENDANTS OF AMOS McGINLEY DEVOR, SON OF JESSE

1   Amos McGinley DEVOR, b. 26 Mar 1832, Spring Run, Franklin Co., PA; d. 20 May 1902; bur. Fannettsburg Cemetery, PA.

Amos m. (1) Margaret BRINLEY. Margaret, dau. of Michael BRINLEY and Catherine KLIPPINGER, b. 9 Oct 1829, d. 6 Dec. 1917; bur. Fannettsburg Cemetery, PA.

    Margaret's father kept a store in Dry Run that later became the Alexander store.
    Amos was a blacksmith and as a smith he had no superior in the valley. He was also a noted teacher of music, a choir director and a member of the Session of the Fannettsburg Presbyterian Church.
    He enlisted in the Civil War as a private on 14 Nov 1864 in Company E of the 82nd Regiment Pennsylvania Volunteers and was discharged on 13 Jul 1865. He participated in the battles of Petersburg and Sailors Creek and was present at the surrender of Lee at Appomattox.

Children:
+   2 M i   John Henderson DEVOR, M.D.
    3 F ii   Tirzah A. DEVOR, b. 25 May 1857.

                Tirzah m. (1) Adam HASHINGER. Adam d. in Kansas City, MO. soon after they were married.

                Tirzah m. (2) Samuel LANTHERS. They lived in Orbisonia, PA, She obtained a life certificate and enjoyed a prominent position among the teachers of Franklin County.

    4 F iii   Nora E. DEVOR, b. 30 Apr 1860; d. 1946; bur. Fannettsburg Cemetery, Fannettsburg,

PA. Nora lived with her sisters Margaret and Cora and did the housework. (Deavor)

5 F   iv   Margaret Susan DEVOR, b. 28 Jul 1862; d. 1946; bur. Fannettsburg Cemetery, Fannettsburg, PA. Margaret was a school teacher with a life certificate. She lived with her sisters Cora and Nora. (Deavor)

+ 6 M   v   Amos McGinley DEVOR, Jr.

7 F   vi   Cora Weldon DEVOR, b. 10 Mar 1859; d. 1931; bur. Fannettsburg Cemetery, Fannettsburg, PA. Cora graduated from Wilson College in June 1892 and was a music teacher. She was adept at vocal and instrumental music. She lived with her sisters Nora and Margaret. (Deavor)

8 M   vii   James DEVOR, b. 17 Aug 1871, Fannettsburg, PA. James was a competent smith and member of the Presbyterian Church. (Deavor)

James m. (1) Ada MILLER.

2   John Henderson DEVOR, M.D., b. 15 Aug 1855, Fannett Twp., or Metal Twp., Franklin Co., PA.
In his boyhood, his parents once lived in Metal Township where he grew up. After local schools, he attended Shippensburg Normal School, took a scientific course and graduated in 1880. Before and while attending college, he taught six years in St. Thomas, Montgomery and Metal Townships and at Mercersburg where he was principal of the public schools. He won laurels as an educator.
He then began the study of medicine with Dr. Zook at Fannettsburg and in 1882 he entered the College of Physicians and Surgeons at Baltimore, graduated in 1885, and located in Fort Loudon. He also took a post graduate course at Poly Clinic Hospital at Philadelphia, PA.
Dr. Devor became the president of the Medical Society and School Director in Deters Township for 2 years.

John m. (1) Ada Beatrice SMITH 11 Apr 1887, Ft. Loudon, PA. Ada, dau. of John SMITH, b. Oct 1866, Ft. Louden, Franklin Co., PA; d. Detroit, Wayne Co., MI.
They were married by Rev. Pomeroy.

Children:
+ 9 M i   Donald Smith DEVOR.
  10 M ii   Jenner Higbee DEVOR, b. 20 May 1891.
  11 M iii William Eugene Henderson DEVOR, b. 26 May
            1894.
  12 F iv   Garnet DEVOR.

6 Amos McGinley DEVOR, Jr., b. 7 Apr 1865.
       Amos was a competent smith and wagon maker.
   (Deavor)

   Amos Jr. m. (1) Nettie ROBINSON.

Children:
   13 F i   Ethel DEVOR.
   14 F ii   Ruth DEVOR.

                    THIRD GENERATION

9 Donald Smith DEVOR, b. 24 Jan 1889, Ft. Louden,
   Franklin Co., PA; d. 11 Aug 1955, Detroit, Wayne Co.,
   MI.

   Donald m. (1) Esther Nora CAMPBELL 31 Oct 1911, State
   College, Centre Co., PA. Esther, dau. of Henry Clay
   CAMPBELL and Jane Ann BAILEY, b. 12 May 1888,
   Fairbrook, PA; d. 29 Dec 1974, New Canaan, Fairfield,
   CT.

Children:
   15 M i   Richard Campbell DEVOR, b. 25 Oct 1927,
             Detroit, Wayne Co., MI.

             Richard m. (1) Mary Ann ROLLINS 17 Nov 1952,
             Nashville, TN.   Mary, b. 30 Oct 1926,
             Nashville, TN.

CHAPTER IV

DESCENDANTS OF JACOB DEAVOR, SON OF JOSEPH

Children of Jacob that left descendants
are listed with their descendants.

The children are:
Martha, James, Annie,
Adam and Hannah

FIRST GENERATION

1 Martha DEAVOR, b. 1 Dec 1800, Taylor Twp., Fulton Co.,
   PA; d. 28 Aug 1865; bur. Clear Ridge, Fulton Co., PA.
        Martha was a faithful member of the M. E. Church
   from early life. (Deavor)

   Martha m. (1) Vincent STEVENS 8 Jan 1824. Vincent, b.
   5 May 1797; d. 25 Oct 1886; bur. Clear Ridge.
        Vincent joined the Methodist Church at age 19 and
   was a class leader and exhorter for most of his life.

Children:
+   2 M   i   James Lane STEVENS.
+   3 M   ii   Philip Deavor STEVENS.
+   4 M   iii Joseph Deavor STEVENS.
+   5 M   iv   Jacob Taylor STEVENS.
+   6 M   v   Rev. Benjamin Fletcher STEVENS.
    7 M   vi   Rev. I. C. STEVENS, b. 15 Feb 1833; d. 29
               Nov 1869; bur. Jersey Shore.
                    Rev. Stevens taught school and attended
               the Cassville Seminary. He entered the
               Baltimore Conference in 1857 and preached
               until his early death. (Deavor)

    8 F   vii Mary J. STEVENS, b. 2 Feb 1835.
               Mary m. (1) Wilson CUTCHALL.
               Children:
               Laura, Collins, John, Mary, Harry, Franklin
               and Sadie CUTCHALL.

    9 F   viii Martha M. STEVENS, b. 1837.
               Martha m. (1) Daniel HEATON. Daniel was a
               school teacher and a shoemaker.
               Children:
               Georgia, Collins, Emma, Will, Mollie,
               Carrie, Guss, Hariett, James and Charles
               HEATON.

+ 10 M ix   John Wesley STEVENS.

SECOND GENERATION

2 James Lane STEVENS, b. 12 Dec 1824. James was a
   druggist in IL.
   James m. Rebecca SIPES.

```
Children:
     11 M i      John Scott STEVENS.
                 John was a lawyer in Chicago.

     12 M ii     George STEVENS.   George was a druggist.

     13 M iii    William STEVENS.
     14 F iv     Olive STEVENS.
     15 F v      Missouri STEVENS.

3  Philip Deavor STEVENS, b. 1 May 1826, Bedford Co., PA.
   Philip m. (1) Susana GREEN 29 Feb.

Children:
     16 M i      James Vincent STEVENS, b. Sep 1848.
                 James m. Elizabeth HOLLAND 4 Jan 1869.

     17 F ii     Mary Jane STEVENS, b. Nov 1850.
                 Mary Jane m. (1) John BERKSTRESSER.

     18 F iii    Juniata Amanda STEVENS, b. 13 Mar 1853; d.
                 1854.

     19 F iv     Florence Lavina STEVENS, b. Sep 1855.
                 Florence m. (1) William ROBINSON.
                 Children:
                 Merrill b. 9 Feb 1876, Homer, Maud, Lillian,
                 Charles, Ivey, and John  ROBINSON.

     20 M v      Lemuel Green STEVENS, b. 26 Jul 1859.

     21 F vi     Elizabeth Alice STEVENS, b. 24 Apr 1862.
                 Elizabeth m. (1) Daniel BENLER.

     22 M vii    Theodore Taylor STEVENS, b. Sep 1863.

     23 F viii   Martha Belle STEVENS, b. Nov 1866.
                 Martha m. (1) Harry SMITH.

     24 M ix     Edward Luther STEVENS, b. 20 Jan 1869; d.
                 1869.

     25 M x      Emory Clark STEVENS, b. Dec 1870.

4  Joseph Deavor STEVENS, b. 26 Sep 1827.
   Joseph m. (1) Hannah HOLLAND 26 Dec 1848.  Hannah d.
   26 Mar 1878; bur. Clear Ridge, PA.

Children:
     26 M i      Thomas B. STEVENS, b. 28 Nov 1839.  Thomas
                 was a carpenter and painter.
```

Thomas m. (1) Ellen HENRY 1871.
Children: All four were Methodists.
Nathan H., Benjamin Edmonson, Hannah
Elizabeth, and Hester Olive STEVENS.

27 M ii   James Dyke STEVENS, b. 19 Apr 1851.

James m. (1) Phoebe KERLIN Mar 1879.
James was a farmer.
Children:
Sarah Alberda and Mertie Emma STEVENS.

28 M iii Vincent C. STEVENS, b. 26 Nov 1852.
Vincent m. (1) Emma COBERT.
Vincent was a teacher. He and Emma were
members of the Methodist Church in Three
Springs.

29 M iv   Isaac STEVENS.
30 M v   John F. STEVENS, M.D., b. 7 Mar 1855.

John m. (1) Gertrude C. WRIGHT 27 Jun 1894.
John taught school for several years and
attended Louisville Medical School. He then
established a medical practice in Kansas.
(Deavor)

31 M vi   Rev. George Washington STEVENS, b. 5 Mar
1857.
George graduated from Dickinson
Seminary in 1881 and was ordained Deacon in
1882 and elder in 1885. He has had 9
ministerial appointments and has had five
churches built or repaired. He has
converted over 1000 souls. As a financier,
preacher and pastor he has few superiors.
(Deavor)

Rev. George m. (1) Clara RAMSEY 22 Feb 1883.
Children:
Nellie Belle, Mary Ray, Bessie May, Carlton
and an unnamed child STEVENS.

32 F vii Emma Frances STEVENS, b. 8 Sep 1859.
Emma m. John SHAFER 1894

33 M viii Albert F. STEVENS, M.D., b. 2 May 1861.
Albert taught school and graduated from the
University of PA. He practiced medicine in
Shelby, IA. (Deavor)
Albert, M.D. m. (1) Lulu LINN 1 Sep 1892.

```
34 M ix    Franklin K. STEVENS, D.D.S., b. 26 Nov 1863.
           Franklin was a teacher and graduated from
           the U. of PA.  He practiced dentistry in
           McConnelsburg, PA.  (Deavor)

           Franklin m. (1) Myra HENRY 1892.  Children:
           Russell STEVENS.
```

Joseph Deavor STEVENS m. (2) Ellen Frances ELIAS 2 Dec 1879.

Children: Edward Gray and Charles Escoe STEVENS.

5   Jacob Taylor STEVENS, b. 24 Apr 1829.
        Jacob was a shoemaker, though crippled for many years. He operated a small notion store in Altoona, PA.

Jacob m. (1) Sarah A. RUTHERFORD 2 May 1850. Sarah, b. 26 Sep 1827; d. 29 Jun 1886.

Children:
```
    35 F i     Rebecca V. STEVENS, b. 2 Feb 1851; d. 1860;
               bur. Jefferson Co., IL.
    36 F ii    Mary E. STEVENS, b. 5 Jan 1853.
               Mary m. (1) William KRIST.

    37 F iii   Margaret STEVENS, b. 11 Apr 1855; d. 17 Feb
               1884.
    38 M iv    William T. STEVENS, b. 23 Oct 1857.  William
               was a blacksmith.
               William m. (1) Mary SNARE.
               William m. (2) Annie HARTZELL.

    39 F v     Elizabeth S. STEVENS, b. 12 May 1860.
               Elizabeth m. (1) Joseph POTTER.
               Elizabeth m. (2) Albert KREPTS.

    40 M vi    Charlie STEVENS, b. 6 Sep 1862.  Charlie was
               a brakeman on the P. R. R. at Altoona, PA.
               Charlie m. (1) Annie ARMSTRONG.  They had
               four children.

    41 F vii   Ida M. STEVENS, b. 4 Dec 1864.
               Ida m. (1) George CAROLOUS.  George was a
               machinist.
               Children:  Curtis and Millard CAROLOUS.

    42 M viii  Samuel STEVENS, b. 4 May 1867; d. 28 Mar
               1868; bur. Houstontown, PA.
```

Jacob m. (2) Miss HOUSEMAN 6 Feb 1889.

Children:
    43 F ix   Lillie Belle STEVENS, b. 18 Jan 1890.

6   Rev. Benjamin Fletcher STEVENS, b. 26 Mar 1831.
        Benjamin united with the M. E. Church at age 18.
    He attended Cassville Seminary and was ordained deacon
    in 1857 and elder in 1859. He had many appointments
    over 35 years and has converted over 1000 souls.
    (Deavor)

    Benjamin m. Harriet G. RHOADS 17 Apr 1861.

Children:
    44 M i   Clubine R. STEVENS.
    45 M ii   John C. STEVENS.
    46 F iii   Annie M. STEVENS.
    47 M iv   William F. STEVENS
    48 F v   Nellie B. STEVENS.

10 John Wesley STEVENS, b. 2 Feb 1839, Wooden Bridge,
    Fulton Co., PA.
        John Wesley was raised on a farm and walked 3
    miles to a school where the term was only 3 months.
    At 18 he attended a special school and became a
    teacher. On Oct 19 1862 he volunteered for Co. H. PA.
    Infantry Regiment. He was discharged and reenlisted
    in 1864 and served until Jun 1865. After the war he
    farmed and learned the shoe trade.

    John m. (1) Margaret Jane McKEAN 29 Sep 1874.

Children:
    49 M i   Andrew STEVENS, b. 30 Jun 1875.
    50 M ii   Vincent STEVENS, b. 30 Jun 1875
    51 M iii   Marion STEVENS, b. 10 Oct 1877; d. 17 Oct
                1877.

DESCENDANTS OF JAMES DEAVOR, SON OF JACOB

FIRST GENERATION

1   James DEAVOR, b. 1811; d. 1888; bur. Fairview Cemetery.
        James farmed some, but followed the trades of cooper and tinner. He became a life long member of the M. E. Church in 1826.

    James m. (1) Hannah STEVENS, b. 1814; d. 1890; bur. Fairview Cemetery.

Children:
     2 F   i   Elizabeth DEAVOR, d. 1864, Mt. Carroll, IL.
+   3 M   ii   Jesse Allen DEAVOR.
     4 F   iii   Mary Ellen DEAVOR, b. 16 Mar 1838.

                 Mary m. (1) Jacob F. SALKIELD 4 Mar 1858.
                 Jacob, d. 11 Mar 1872, Crossfield, PA; bur.
                 Centre, PA
                 Children:
                 Alice, Albert, Sarah, John, Hannah and
                 Franklin SALKIELD.

     5 F   iv   Martha Rebecca DEAVOR, b. 13 Dec 1840, West
                 Dublin, PA.

                 Martha m. (1) Samuel Wesley SALKIELD 7 Aug
                 1862. Samuel, b. 2 Jun 1839, Ft. Littleton,
                 PA.

+   6 M   v   John Minnich DEAVOR.
     7 F   vi   Sarah Ann DEAVOR.
+   8 M   vii   Josiah Vincent DEAVOR.

SECOND GENERATION

3   Jesse Allen DEAVOR, d. 1883, Warriors Mark, PA; bur. Warriors Mark, PA.
        Jesse served as a Physician in the Union Army and was a successful doctor at Warriors Mark, PA. He died there of consumption.

    Jesse m. (1) Elizabeth MILLER.

Children:
     9 F   i   Olive DEAVOR, b. abe 1860; d. KS; bur. KS.
                 She died of consumption.

```
    10 F ii    Ida Carey DEAVOR.    Ida graduated from
               Dickinson Seminary in 1887 and prepared for
               missionary work in India.

6  John Minnich DEAVOR, d. 22 Feb 1872; bur. Fairview,
   PA.
   John m. (1) Elizabeth LAMBERSON 14 Feb 1870.

Children:
    11 F i     Bertha DEAVOR, b. Mar 1871.

8  Josiah Vincent DEAVOR.   Josiah was a member of the
   M.E.Church and a long time Justice of the Peace.  He
   farmed the old homestead and had a great interest in
   public education.

   Josiah m. (1) Mary E. LAIDIG 27 Jun 1876.

Children:
    12 M i     John Newell DEAVOR, b. 8 Oct 1877.
    13 M ii    Charles Webster DEAVOR, b. 1879.
    14 F iii   Frances Rebecca DEAVOR, b. 25 Oct 1880.
    15 M iv    Samuel Elmer DEAVOR, b. Mar 1883.
    16 F v     Sarah Elizabeth DEAVOR, b. 7 Jun 1888.
    17 M vi    Ernest Grant DEAVOR, b. 2 Mar 1890.
    18 M vii   Josiah Allen DEAVOR, b. Sep 1892.
    19 M viii  Russell Ellsworth DEAVOR, b. Nov 1894.
```

DESCENDANTS OF ANNIE DEAVOR, DAUGHTER OF JACOB

FIRST GENERATION

```
1  Annie DEAVOR, b. 17 Mar 1814, Trough Creek, PA; d. Jun
   1858; bur. Hartman Chapel.

   Annie m. (1) Jacob LAMBERSON  May 1837.
   Jacob d. 10 apr 1879; bur. Hartman Chapel.


Children:
    2 M   i     Samuel LAMBERSON.
    3 M   ii    Daniel LAMBERSON.
    4 F   iii   Ellen LAMBERSON.
```

DESCENDANTS OF ADAM DEAVOR, SON OF JACOB

FIRST GENERATION

1   Adam DEAVOR, b. 3 Jun 1816, Trough Creek, PA.
          Adam was the father of the author of "A BRIEF
     HISTORY OF THE DEAVOR FAMILY IN AMERICA".
     Adam was born at Trough Creek Valley, PA in a cabin
     that had been erected during the Revolutionary War.
     He lived in the day when there were no free schools
     and he attended Mt. Pleasant School for several
     sessions that totaled only six months.
          Adam was a carpenter, shoemaker, cooper, and
     mason. He owned and operated a shop and sold products
     to his neighbors and never collected their debts by
     law.   He   was   a   Methodist   and   an   advocate   of
     temperance.
          Just prior to his marriage, Adam lived with
     Daniel Laidig, just 20 miles from the home of Angeline
     Yingling at Coles Valley.   Eighteen inches of snow
     fell on the scheduled wedding day but Adam walked the
     20 miles to Angeline's house.   They decided to
     postpone the wedding for two days, so Adam walked back
     home.   On the wedding day a friend took Adam to
     Angeline's by a sled drawn by oxen.   As they came to
     the house two hunters arrived dragging a deer through
     the snow.   After the wedding they had a venison feast
     and Adam and Angeline traveled by ox sled to Laidig's
     where they began house keeping.
          Over the next nineteen years Adam and Angeline
     lived at eight different locations.   Then Adam bought
     three acres at Pleasant Grove and built a home.   He
     also constructed a shop and worked at his trades.
     Angeline died here in 1880 and in 1896 when his son
     William wrote his book Adam was still strong and
     working in his shop.   (Deavor)

     Adam DEAVOR m. (1) Angeline YINGLING 16 Dec 1840,
     Coles Valley, PA.   Angeline, daughter of Peter
     YINGLING and Susanna COFFERSMITH, b. 12 Dec 1822,
     Westminster, MD; d. 29 Feb 1880; bur. Centre, Fulton
     Co., PA.
          Angeline was converted to the Methodist Church as
     a small girl.   She lived with her parents in a
     comfortable Maryland residence but an unfortunate
     business transaction caused the loss of the family
     fortune and the entire family of ten walked 100 miles
     to Hunt Co., PA to a new home.
          Angeline learned to speak English, read and write
     after grown to womanhood.

Children:
+ 2 M   i   Benjamin Alexander Lyon DEAVOR.
+ 3 M   ii   Rev. Ephrain Edward Allen DEAVOR.
+ 4 F   iii Mary Ann Elizabeth Taylor DEAVOR.
+ 5 F   iv   Sarah Ellen Roles DEAVOR.
+ 6 M   v   Rev. Joseph Walter Dyke DEAVOR.
   7 F   vi   Moleno Dell Ray DEAVOR, b. 2 Oct 1856.
              Moleno had a common school education
              and taught school with success. At one time
              she had an attack of quinsy that developed
              into nervous hysteria in which she lost
              sight, hearing and speech for several
              months. Her mother took care of her and in
              return she took care of her mother in her
              last illness and maintained a home for her
              father.

              Moleno m. (1) William C. McLAINE 22 Mar
              1887. William, b. 5 May 1853.
              Children:
              Hazel McLAINE.

+ 8 M   vii James Asbury Collins DEAVOR.
   9 M   viii Jacob Elmer Emerson DEAVOR, b. 3 Mar 1862,
              Fulton Co., PA. Jacob was a blacksmith.

              Jacob m. (1) Maggie H. BERKSTRESSER 23 Oct
              1883, Waterfall, PA.

+ 10 M ix   William Tecumseh Sherman DEAVOR.
   11 M x   Tennyson Loraine DEAVOR, b. 10 Jan 1869,
              Fulton Co., PA. He graduated from
              Bloomsburg State Normal School and became a
              teacher. His writings and poems show
              literary talent.

                    SECOND GENERATION

2. Benjamin Alexander Lyon DEAVOR, b. 7 May 1843.
        Benjamin enlisted in the 58th Reg. Co. A PA.
Volunteers on 29 Sep 1864 and served until 5 Jun 1865.
He was a Methodist, a shoemaker, a carpenter and a
millwright. "His mill on Wooden Bridge Creek was not
surpassed in the State." He was a prohibitionist and
an advocate of public schools. He honorably filled
elective offices.

Benjamin m. (1) Nancy Elizabeth KING 13 Nov 1866.
Nancy, b. 22 Jun 1847, West Dublin, PA.

Children:
```
12 F i    Ida Frances DEAVOR, b. 25 Sep 1867.

          Ida m. (1) A. C. S. HEATON 23 Jan 1887,
          Holidaysburg, PA.
          Children:
          Harvey, George, and Eugene HEATON.

13 M ii   William Edward DEAVOR, b. 7 Sep 1877, Clear
          Ridge, PA.
14 M iii  John Franklin DEAVOR, b. 3 Oct 1886.
```

3 Rev. Ephrian Edward Allen DEAVOR, b. 31 Dec 1845.
        He taught school for several years and then
entered and graduated from Dickinson Seminary. He was
licensed to preach in 1865, was ordained a Deacon in
1874 and ordained elder in 1876. He then served as a
minister and in 1889 received his Ph.D. from Illinois
Wesleyan U. He was a pioneer of self education and a
strong revivalist. He was the first member of his
conference to do post graduate work.
        During his career three churches and two
parsonages were built or repaired and 1200 people were
converted.

Ephrian m. (1) Sue STOTLER 11 Nov 1871, Chewsville,
MO. Sue, b. 21 Jul 1849, Williamsport, MD.

Children:
```
15 M i    Orlando Guy Livingstone DEAVOR, b. 6 Oct
          1876, Wrightsville, PA; d. 14 Mar 1877; bur.
          Fairview Cemetery, Wrightsville, PA.

16 F ii   Elsie Ray DEAVOR, b. 9 Feb 1879,
          Wrightsville, PA.

17 F iii  Josie Pearl DEAVOR, b. 8 Jun 1882, Newton
          Hamilton, PA.
```

4 Mary Ann Elizabeth Taylor DEAVOR, b. 31 Jul 1848, New
Granada, PA.

Mary m. (1) Andrew S. CHILCOAT 19 May 1872. Andrew,
b. 12 Jun 1838.

Children:
```
18 M i    Jessie Allen CHILCOAT, b. 12 Jan 1875.
19 M ii   Howard CHILCOAT, b. 25 Jul 1877.
20 F iii  Dellie Elizabeth CHILCOAT, b. 3 Sep 1880.
21 M iv   Joseph CHILCOAT, b. 2 Aug 1882.
```

5 Sarah Ellen Roles DEAVOR, b. 5 Apr 1852, Bunker Hill, PA.

Sarah m. (1) Michael LAIDIG 8 May 1872. Michael, b. 16 Jul 1852.

Children:
    22 M i   Andrew LAIDIG.
    23 M ii   Edward Arlington LAIDIG, b. 16 Jul 1878.
    24 F iii   Elsie Del Ray LAIDIG, b. 18 Dec 1884.

6 Rev. Joseph Walter Dyke DEAVOR, b. 31 May 1853.
       Joseph was first a school teacher. He graduated from Shippensburg State Normal School in 1876 and received his A.B. degree at Dickinson Seminary in 1880 and served as minister. He obtained his Ph.D. from Illinois Wesleyan U. in 1895. He was an outstanding financier and repaired or built ten churches.

Joseph m (1) Laura Belle McDOWELL 9 Mar 1884, Birmingham, PA. Laura, b. 9 Oct 1860, Newton Hamilton, PA.

Children:
    25 F i   Verna Alice DEAVOR, b. 6 Feb 1885.
    26 F ii   Ruth Lee DEAVOR, b. 29 May 1889.

8 James Asbury Collins DEAVOR, b. 29 Apr 1859.
       James was a farmer and a carpenter.

James m. (1) Sadie E. GROVE 11 Apr 1887. Sadie, b. 12 May 1865, Ft. Littleton, PA.

Children:
    27 M i   James Oscar Clarence DEAVOR, b. 14 Aug 1888.
    28 M ii   Joseph William Warren DEAVOR, b. 23 Apr 1891.
    29 M iii   Amon Elton Lloyd DEAVOR, b. 24 Dec 1893.

10 William Tecumseh Sherman DEAVOR, b. 8 Dec 1864.
       William was named after General William Tecumseh Sherman. In his childhood he had the use of his father's shop and learned to make sleds, wagons, boxes, bowguns and other toys.
       He graduated from Bloomsburg State Normal in 1886 and from Williamsport Dickinson Seminary in 1888. He took his Ph.D. at Allegheny College in 1892. He worked as a teacher and then as a minister and became a professor at St. Johns College, Annapolis, MD in 1892. He published his history of the Deavor Family in 1896 after five years of visiting, or writing to, Deavors and researching public records and cemeteries.

William m. (1) Katie TOTTEN 22 Jan 1891, Northunberland Co., PA. Katie, b. 22 Jan 1871, Wapwallopen, PA.

Children:
```
30 M  i      Randolph Foster DEAVOR, b. 6 Jun 1892.
```


DESCENDANTS OF HANNAH DEAVOR, DAUGHTER OF JACOB

FIRST GENERATION

1 Hannah DEAVOR, b. 27 Feb 1819, Trough Creek, PA. Hannah m. Peter DYKE 4 Dec 1845.

Children:
```
2 F   i      Mary DYKE.
3 F   ii     Sarah DYKE.
4 M   iii    Henry DYKE.
5 M   iv     Peter DYKE, Jr.
```

Hannah m. (2) Jacob CROMER.

Children:
```
6 M   v      Elisha CROMER.
7 F   vi     Elizabeth CROMER.
8 F   vii    Rachel CROMER.
```

"THE DESCENDANTS OF JOSEPH DEVOR
OF PATH VALLEY, PENNSYLVANIA"

The parenthetical names throughout
the book indicates the sources.

PUBLISHED SOURCES

(Deavor) "A BRIEF HISTORY OF THE DEAVOR FAMILY IN
AMERICA" by Rev. William T. S. Deavor, M.E.Book Rooms
Print, Harrisburg, PA, 1896.

(Mann) "THE DEVORE/DE VORE FAMILIES" by Betty M. Mann,
Woolworth Publishing Co., Hillsdale, MI.

(Hawley Society) "DESCENDANTS OF PETER HAWLEY OF
MONTGOMERY COUNTY, VIRGINIA" by the Society of the
Hawley Family, Inc., Heritage Books, Inc., Bowie, MD,
1997.

(Richard) "THE ANCESTRY AND DESCENDANTS OF JOHN
GROSVENOR OF ROXBURY, MASSACHUSETTS" by Richard
Grosvenor, Heritage Books, Inc., Bowie, MD, 1997.

UNPUBLISHED MANUSCRIPTS

(Corwin) "DEVOR FAMILY" by Corwin Johnston, 10 pages,
1949.

(Philip) "DESCENDANTS OF MARTIN LAWRENCE HAMMOND" by
Philip Lawrence Hammond, 1981.

(Zella) Pedigree of Cecil Hart Devor by Zella Devor
Forrester.

LETTERS

(Corwin) 1951 Letter from Corwin Johnston to Zella
Forrester.

(Cora) May 18, 1975 Letter from Cora Devor Wearin
listing descendants of David Devor.

LETTERS TO ANNA HAWLEY GROSVENOR

(Mary) Many letters from Mary Takach Devor.

(Juanita) Juanita Devor Kaltenbaugh.

(Wearin) James Wearin about his family, 1998.

(Beulah) Beulah Devor Spann about her family, 1998.

DOCUMENTS IN POSSESSION OF ANNA GROSVENOR

Bible of Jacob J. Devor containing Devor family records printed in 1872 at Philadelphia by William W. Harding.

Joseph Deavor's Certificate of Military Service, 1780.

Chester County, PA Tax Record for Joseph Deavor, 1780.

Diary and poems of Nora Grace Hawley.

VITAL STATISTICS CERTIFICATES

Birth Certificates:
   Solomon Warren Crouse
   Sarah Ann Devor
   Anna May Hawley
   Richard B. Grosvenor
   Susan Mae Grosvenor

Marriage Certificates:
   Solomon Warren Crouse and Sarah Ann Devor
   Miller H. Hawley and Carrie E. Devor

Marriage License:
   Richard Browne Grosvenor and Anna Mae Hawley
   licensed to be joined in marriage, 5 May 1943.

Death Certificates:
   Miller Henry Hawley
   Carrie Ethel Devor Hawley

Certificates of Baptism:
   Anna May Hawley
   Nora Grace Hawley
   Betty Lois Hawley
   Dorothy Jean Grosvenor
   Susan Mae Grosvenor

Cemetery Deed:
   Carrie Devor Hawley

OTHER SOURCES

(Lilah) Oral information from Lilah Wearin Johnson.

INDEX

Family Name	Given Name, Birth Date	Pages
ADAM	Carl J.	35
ADAMS	Margaret	71
AMES	Helen Gail	87
ANDERSON	Diane, 1959	46
APPLEBY	W. M., M.D.	14
ARMSTRONG	Annie	102
BAILEY	Jane Ann	96
BAKER	(____)	8
BAKER	Anna Sarah	38
BARR	Mary	14
BARRETT	Pamela	46
BATCHILDER	Blanch	50
BATES	Fannie	48
BAXTER	Kathryn	40
BENLER	Daniel	100
BERKS	George	13
BERKSTRESSER	John	100
BERKSTRESSER	Maggie H	107
BIBBINS	Charles	19
BIEBER	Leah Amelia	86
BLACK	Sarah	15
BLAIR	Margaret	32
BOHNENKAMP	Henry A.	25
BOHNENKAMP	Vincent Henry, 1923	25
BONNER	Frank	39
BONNIE	Frank	39
BOYER	Albert, 1894	12
BOYER	Dorothy	12
BOYER	Lawrence	12
BOYER	Sadie A., 1866	20
BRADY	Joan	61
BRANDT	Mary Ann	32
BRIGGS	Mary, 1899	41
BRINDLE	Margaret	69
BRINDLEY	Jacob	65
BRINDLEY	Michael	65
BRINLEY	Elizabeth, 1831	65
BRINLEY	Jacob	65
BRINLEY	Margaret, 1829	94
BRINLEY	Michael	94
BRINOR	Rev. C. F.	69

INDEX

Family Name	Given Name, Birth Date	Pages

Family Name	Given Name, Birth Date	Pages
BROWN	Hannah	15
BURKE	Hannah Jane "Jennie"	32
BURKE	James	32
BURKET	Mary Ellen	73
BUTTS	Paul	39
BYERS	Rosa Lee	55
CABLE	Donald	37
CABLE	Harry E.	37
CABLE	Jean	37
CABLE	Nelda	37
CABLE	Richard	37
CALHOUN	Deborah May, 1962	83
CALHOUN	Gregory Grant "Greg", 1964	83
CALHOUN	Harry Grant	82
CAMPBELL	Brendan	33
CAMPBELL	Cara Elizabeth, 1984	33
CAMPBELL	Esther Nora, 1888	96
CAMPBELL	Henry Clay	96
CAMPBELL	Jack Crouse, 1922	33
CAMPBELL	Jane	36
CAMPBELL	Linda Mae, 1951	33
CAMPBELL	Lyle Crouse, M.D., 1950	33
CAMPBELL	Lyle Wood	32
CAMPBELL	Ross	73
CAMPBELL	William Alexander	32
CAMPER	Lottie	25
CARBAUGH	Alma	23
CARBAUGH	Augustus	24
CARBAUGH	Brian Allen, 1974	92
CARBAUGH	Daniel	88
CARBAUGH	David Frank	88
CARBAUGH	David Frank, 1945	91
CARBAUGH	Frank	88
CARBAUGH	Frank Edward, 1921	88
CARBAUGH	Jeri Lynn, 1946	91
CARBAUGH	Laurie Ann, 1972	91
CARBAUGH	Susan	24
CAROLOUS	Curtis	102
CAROLOUS	George	102
CAROLOUS	Millard	102
CARPENTER	John L.	38

INDEX

Family Name	Given Name, Birth Date	Pages
CHALK	Frank, 1897	53
CHALK	Jim	53
CHAPMAN	Alice	86
CHAPPIS	Marie, 1926	25
CHILCOAT	Andrew S., 1838	108
CHILCOAT	Dellie Elizabeth, 1880	108
CHILCOAT	Howard, 1877	108
CHILCOAT	Jesse Allen, 1875	108
CHILCOAT	Joseph, 1882	108
CHOLOWINSKI	Edward	90
CHOLOWINSKI	Norman, 1956	90
CLARK	Rachel	5
CLARK	Walter	14
CLARKE	Jane	36
CLARKE	William	35
CLAVER	Mr.	8
CLIPPINGER	Catherine	94
CLIPPINGER	Catherine "Kitty", 1831	65
CLIPPINGER	Gill	39
CLUGSTON	Myrtle, 1905	47
COBERT	Emma	101
COCHRAN	Daniel Ezra, 1860	15
COCHRAN	Ely	15
COCHRAN	John	15
COCHRAN	Minnie	15
COCHRAN	Rosena	15
COCHRAN	Virgil	15
COCHRAN	Wallace	15
COFFERSMITH	Susanna	106
COLEMAN	Nellie, 1861	22
COOK	Merle	52
CORNETT	Jenny	63
CORTEZ	Herman	63
CORTEZ	Nathan	63
COTTON	John	18
COTTON	Willis	18
COURSON	James	58
COWDEN	Marilyn Ann, 1952	44
COWDEN	Wilmer, 1916	44
CRAMER	Mariah	34, 69
CROMER	Elisha	110

INDEX

Family Name	Given Name, Birth Date	Pages
CROMER	Elizabeth	110
CROMER	Jacob	110
CROMER	Rachel	110
CROUSE	Bertha "Bertie"	30
CROUSE	Ed	30
CROUSE	Elizabeth	36
CROUSE	Ellen	35
CROUSE	George	30
CROUSE	John Dallas	31
CROUSE	John Dallas, 1847	32
CROUSE	Mabel Zelda	32
CROUSE	Sarah B.	29
CROUSE	Solomon B.	30, 73
CROUSE	Solomon Warren "Sol"	30, 73
CROUSE	Solomon Warren "Sol", 1885	31
CROUSE	Stella	30
CROUSE	Stella, 1881	31
CROUSE	William	30
CROUSE	William West, 1870	32
CROUSE	William, 1821	31
CROY	Aletha Jane	91
CRYTZER	Ruth	78, 79
CULBERSON	Sarah, 1853	11
CUTCHALL	Collins	99
CUTCHALL	Franklin	99
CUTCHALL	Harry	99
CUTCHALL	John	99
CUTCHALL	Laura	99
CUTCHALL	Mary	99
CUTCHALL	Sadie	99
CUTCHALL	Wilson	99
DAVER	Jesse	3
DAVER	Jesse, 1771	6
DAVER	Joseph 1745	3
DAVIS	Annie	14
DAVIS	Blanche Roberson	62
DAVIS	Jack	62
DAVIS	Susan Leann	62
DEAVOR	Adam	7
DEAVOR	Adam, 1816	106
DEAVOR	Amon Elton Lloyd, 1893	109

INDEX

Family Name	Given Name, Birth Date	Pages
DEAVOR	Annie	7
DEAVOR	Annie, 1814	105
DEAVOR	Benjamin Alexander Lyon	107
DEAVOR	Benjamin Alexander Lyon, 1843	107
DEAVOR	Bertha, 1871	105
DEAVOR	Charles Webster, 1879	105
DEAVOR	Elizabeth	104
DEAVOR	Elsie Ray, 1879	108
DEAVOR	Ernest Grant, 1890	105
DEAVOR	Esther	7
DEAVOR	Frances Rebecca, 1880	105
DEAVOR	Hannah	7
DEAVOR	Hannah, 1819	110
DEAVOR	Ida Carey	105
DEAVOR	Ida Frances, 1867	108
DEAVOR	Jacob	3, 7
DEAVOR	Jacob Elmer Emerson, 1862	107
DEAVOR	James	7
DEAVOR	James Asbury Collins, 1859	109
DEAVOR	James Oscar Clarence, 1888	109
DEAVOR	James, 1811	104
DEAVOR	Jesse	7
DEAVOR	Jesse Allen	104
DEAVOR	John Franklin, 1886	108
DEAVOR	John Minnich	104,105
DEAVOR	John Newell, 1877	105
DEAVOR	Joseph William Warren, 1891	109
DEAVOR	Joseph, 1745	3
DEAVOR	Joseph, 1804	7
DEAVOR	Josiah Allen, 1892	105
DEAVOR	Josiah Vincent	104,105
DEAVOR	Josie Pearl, 1882	108
DEAVOR	Martha	7
DEAVOR	Martha Rebecca, 1840	104
DEAVOR	Martha, 1800	99
DEAVOR	Mary Ann Elizabeth Taylor	107
DEAVOR	Mary Ann Elizabeth Taylor, 1848	108
DEAVOR	Mary Ellen, 1838	104
DEAVOR	Mary, 1806	7
DEAVOR	Moleno Dell Ray, 1856	107
DEAVOR	Olive, 1860	104

INDEX

Family Name	Given Name, Birth Date	Pages
DEAVOR	Orlando Guy Livingston, 1876	108
DEAVOR	Philip Piles	7
DEAVOR	Randolph Foster, 1892	110
DEAVOR	Rev. Ephrain Edward Alllen	107
DEAVOR	Rev. Ephrian Edward Allen, 1845	108
DEAVOR	Rev. Joseph Walter Dyke	107
DEAVOR	Rev. Joseph Walter Dyke, 1853	109
DEAVOR	Russell Ellsworth, 1894	105
DEAVOR	Ruth Lee, 1889	109
DEAVOR	Samuel Elmer, 1883	105
DEAVOR	Sarah Ann	104
DEAVOR	Sarah Elizabeth 1888	105
DEAVOR	Sarah Ellen Roles, 1852	109
DEAVOR	Sarah Elllen Roles	107
DEAVOR	Tennyson Lorain, 1869	107
DEAVOR	Verna Alice, 1885	109
DEAVOR	William Edward, 1877	108
DEAVOR	William Tecumseh Sherman	107,109
DEFREES	Elizabeth M	18
DESKINS	Connie, 1949	91
DESKINS	Minor Harvey	91
DEVOR	Agnes	12
DEVOR	Agnes Jane	14
DEVOR	Agnes, 1823	13
DEVOR	Albert, 1873	23
DEVOR	Albino	3, 4
DEVOR	Alice Ann, 1854	15
DEVOR	Allie, 1917	53
DEVOR	Alyce Kay, 1934	80
DEVOR	Ambrose, 1889	23
DEVOR	Amos F., 1903	52
DEVOR	Amos McGinley	6
DEVOR	Amos McGinley, 1832	94
DEVOR	Amos McGinley, Jr.	95
DEVOR	Amos McGinley, Jr., 1865	96
DEVOR	Ann	5
DEVOR	Anna Susan	66
DEVOR	Anna Susan, 1866	71
DEVOR	Annie	47
DEVOR	Ardella, 1891	23
DEVOR	Arthur Abraham	50

INDEX

Family Name	Given Name, Birth Date	Pages
DEVOR	Arthur Abraham, 1880	53
DEVOR	Arthur Agnew	54
DEVOR	Arthur Agnew, 1906	57
DEVOR	Arthur William	53, 57
DEVOR	Basil J., 1829	21
DEVOR	Bathsheba, aft 1813	12
DEVOR	Betty, 1925	53
DEVOR	Beulah Mae	54
DEVOR	Beulah Mae, 1917	59
DEVOR	Blanche	80
DEVOR	Bobby	57
DEVOR	Bradford, 1875	23
DEVOR	Bradley, 1970	61
DEVOR	Caroline, 1840	22
DEVOR	Carrie	6
DEVOR	Carrie Ethel	70
DEVOR	Carrie Ethel, 1889	73
DEVOR	Catherine M. D., 1842	22
DEVOR	Catherine Naomi, 1896	23
DEVOR	Catherine, 1820	12, 13
DEVOR	Catherine, abt 1812	5
DEVOR	Cecil Hart	50, 57
DEVOR	Cecil Hart, 1883	54
DEVOR	Cecil Hart, Jr.	54
DEVOR	Cecil Hart, Jr., 1910	58
DEVOR	Cecil Wilklow	53
DEVOR	Charleen	58
DEVOR	Charles A., 1850	14
DEVOR	Charles Wesley	54
DEVOR	Charles Wesley, 1912	58
DEVOR	Claude Ernest 1884	51
DEVOR	Clyde M., 1885	17
DEVOR	Cora Elizabeth	52
DEVOR	Cora Elizabeth, 1897	55
DEVOR	Cora Weldon, 1859	95
DEVOR	Cornelia	20
DEVOR	Craig, 1970	61
DEVOR	David A., 1893	17
DEVOR	David H.	6
DEVOR	David H., 1825	48
DEVOR	David Herron	14

INDEX

Family Name	Given Name, Birth Date	Pages
DEVOR	David Herron, 1824	15
DEVOR	David S., 1857	23
DEVOR	David Sherman, 1865	15
DEVOR	David, 1914	53
DEVOR	Donald R.	71
DEVOR	Donald Smith	96
DEVOR	Donald Smith, 1889	96
DEVOR	Doras	66
DEVOR	Doras McGinley	31
DEVOR	Doras McGinley, 1861	69
DEVOR	Doris Marybelle	53
DEVOR	Doris, 1923	25
DEVOR	Dorothy, 1921	25
DEVOR	Earl Raphel, 1896	24
DEVOR	Earl, 1889	22
DEVOR	Edith Jane, 1892	23
DEVOR	Eleanor, abt. 1770	3
DEVOR	Elias	15
DEVOR	Elias, 1846	22
DEVOR	Elias, 1856	16
DEVOR	Elinor, 1899	16
DEVOR	Elizabeth	3, 21
DEVOR	Elizabeth Catherine, 1834	14
DEVOR	Elizabeth J., 1910	47
DEVOR	Elizabeth Laird "Lizzie"	48, 49
DEVOR	Elizabeth Lavina, 1839	18
DEVOR	Elizabeth, 1829	6
DEVOR	Elmer W., 1893	17
DEVOR	Emma Lease	22
DEVOR	Emma Orio, 1852	19
DEVOR	Emma Rebecca, 1826	18
DEVOR	Erica, 1978	89
DEVOR	Esther	3
DEVOR	Ethel	96
DEVOR	Ethelyn, 1892	20
DEVOR	Eugene B., 1896	16
DEVOR	Eva, 1895	17
DEVOR	Fanny	20
DEVOR	Fay, 1896	17
DEVOR	Flora Ellen, 1856	19
DEVOR	Forest A., 1893	16

INDEX

Family Name	Given Name, Birth Date	Pages
DEVOR	Frances Ella May, 1892	24
DEVOR	Francy, 1967	88
DEVOR	Frank E., 1890	16
DEVOR	Frank S.	48
DEVOR	Frank S., 1877	52
DEVOR	Frank Starr	19
DEVOR	Frank Starr	20
DEVOR	Frank, 1920	53
DEVOR	Galen Leslie, 1889	68
DEVOR	Garnet	96
DEVOR	Gates Elmore Ellsworth	23, 24
DEVOR	George	53
DEVOR	Gerald L., 1858	22
DEVOR	Gertie B., 1884	17
DEVOR	Gladys	89
DEVOR	Gladys Ada, 1934	80
DEVOR	Gladys Viola	71
DEVOR	Gladys Viola, 1910	81
DEVOR	Goldie O., 1885	16
DEVOR	Hannah	5, 21
DEVOR	Hannah Ellen, 1868	15
DEVOR	Hannah, 1788	11
DEVOR	Harry C.	21
DEVOR	Harry Harvey, 1873	15
DEVOR	Hazel, 1912	52
DEVOR	Helen Agnes "Nellie", 1883	51
DEVOR	Herbert	57
DEVOR	Horace L.	15
DEVOR	Howard	53
DEVOR	Huldah Eleanor, 1872	67
DEVOR	Iva	53
DEVOR	J. Edward, 1827	21
DEVOR	Jacob A.	15
DEVOR	Jacob A., 1870	17
DEVOR	Jacob J.	6
DEVOR	Jacob J., 1827	65
DEVOR	Jacob Peter, 1822	14
DEVOR	Jacob Porter, 1859	15
DEVOR	James	3
DEVOR	James 1765	5
DEVOR	James Edgar	15

INDEX

Family Name	Given Name, Birth Date	Pages
DEVOR	James Edgar, 1869	16
DEVOR	James H.	6
DEVOR	James H., 1822	48
DEVOR	James Rolland, 1834	18
DEVOR	James, 1801	21
DEVOR	James, 1871	95
DEVOR	James, Jr.	5
DEVOR	Jane	6, 47
DEVOR	Jane, 1816	29
DEVOR	Jemima	5
DEVOR	Jemima, 1796	13
DEVOR	Jenner Higbee, 1891	96
DEVOR	Jenny	21
DEVOR	Jerel	59, 61
DEVOR	Jesse	47
DEVOR	Jesse Eugene	71
DEVOR	Jesse Eugene, 1907	78
DEVOR	Jessie Catherine, 1871	66
DEVOR	John	5, 20
DEVOR	John Abraham, 1920	54
DEVOR	John C.	16
DEVOR	John D.	18
DEVOR	John D., 1836	20
DEVOR	John Elmer, 1863	66
DEVOR	John Elmer, 1884	70
DEVOR	John Henderson, M.D.	94
DEVOR	John Henderson, M.D., 1855	95
DEVOR	John R.	15
DEVOR	John T., 1854	15
DEVOR	John Wesley	80
DEVOR	John Wesley, 1901	50
DEVOR	John William	48,57,66
DEVOR	John William, 1857	49
DEVOR	John, 1796	13
DEVOR	John, 1860	23
DEVOR	Joseph	5, 6
DEVOR	Joseph 1745	3
DEVOR	Joseph Clement, 1900	52
DEVOR	Joseph Defrees	18
DEVOR	Joseph Defrees, 1828	19
DEVOR	Joseph Eldon	54

INDEX

Family Name	Given Name, Birth Date	Pages
DEVOR	Joseph Eldon, 1914	58
DEVOR	Joseph Henry	48
DEVOR	Joseph Henry, 1859	50
DEVOR	Joseph Mansfield	24
DEVOR	Joseph Mansfield, 1896	25
DEVOR	Joseph, 1793	12
DEVOR	Joseph, 1820	47
DEVOR	Joseph, 1871	23
DEVOR	Joshua Lafayette	16
DEVOR	Joshua Lafayette, 1859	17
DEVOR	Joshua, Rev.	5
DEVOR	Juanita Alice	70
DEVOR	Juanita Alice, 1893	76
DEVOR	Karen	57
DEVOR	Katherine Laura "Belle", 1890	24
DEVOR	Kathy	58
DEVOR	Kathy, 1960	88
DEVOR	Kelly Kristine, 1976	89
DEVOR	Kenneth	57
DEVOR	Leah, 1868	23
DEVOR	Lemuel, 1837	22
DEVOR	Lizzie Ida	22
DEVOR	Lori, 1973	61
DEVOR	Lucille Zella, 1857	16
DEVOR	Luetta May, 1868	72
DEVOR	Luetta May	66
DEVOR	Lydia	5,23,26
DEVOR	Mabel	53
DEVOR	Margaret "Maggie"	21
DEVOR	Margaret Ellen	65
DEVOR	Margaret Elllen, 1850	67
DEVOR	Margaret Susan, 1862	95
DEVOR	Margaret, 1848	22
DEVOR	Marianette, 1864	19
DEVOR	Marion	58
DEVOR	Marion, 1906	52
DEVOR	Marshall B., 1897	16
DEVOR	Martin G., 1853	47
DEVOR	Martin, 1891	70
DEVOR	Mary "Mollie"	48, 52
DEVOR	Mary	3,6,48,57

INDEX

Family Name	Given Name, Birth Date	Pages
DEVOR	Mary Agnes, 1864	15
DEVOR	Mary Alice	59, 61
DEVOR	Mary Ann	21 ,59
DEVOR	Mary Annette, 1831	18
DEVOR	Mary Elizabeth	65
DEVOR	Mary Elizabeth, 1854	69
DEVOR	Mary Elizabeth, 1894	24
DEVOR	Mary Ellen, 1920	54
DEVOR	Mary, 1818	34
DEVOR	Mary, 1866	23
DEVOR	Mary, 1894	24
DEVOR	Melinda Jane, 1854	16
DEVOR	Michael G	77
DEVOR	Michael G., 1948	88
DEVOR	Milton V., 1854	19
DEVOR	Nancy	3
DEVOR	Nancy E., 1897	16
DEVOR	Nancy May, 1875	16
DEVOR	Nancy, 1838	22
DEVOR	Nora E., 1860	94
DEVOR	Opal Ruth	52
DEVOR	Opal Ruth, 1888	54
DEVOR	Orie M., 1889	20
DEVOR	Pansy, 1909	52
DEVOR	Patricia	57
DEVOR	Paul Edgar,	16
DEVOR	Phebe J., 1899	17
DEVOR	Rachel Fiester	48
DEVOR	Rachel Fiester, 1855	49
DEVOR	Ralph Winfield, 1882	51
DEVOR	Ray, 1884	22
DEVOR	Rev. William Mackey	65
DEVOR	Rev. William Mackey, 1852	68
DEVOR	Richard Augustus "Lloyd" 1889	24
DEVOR	Richard Campbell, 1927	96
DEVOR	Richard M.	22, 26
DEVOR	Richard M., 1831/1833	23
DEVOR	Richard M/E	5, 26
DEVOR	Richard M/E, 1803	22
DEVOR	Rilla Ermina	54
DEVOR	Rilla Ermina, 1908	58

INDEX

Family Name	Given Name, Birth Date	Pages
DEVOR	Rolland	5
DEVOR	Rolland H., 1883	16
DEVOR	Rolland, 1800	18
DEVOR	Ronald W.	77
DEVOR	Ronald W., 1940	88
DEVOR	Rosalie	59
DEVOR	Ruemma, 1901	52
DEVOR	Ruth	96
DEVOR	Ruth E., 1893	17
DEVOR	Samuel	15
DEVOR	Sarah Ann	70
DEVOR	Sarah Ann, 1887	31, 73
DEVOR	Sarah Elizabeth, 1859	15
DEVOR	Serepta Jane	65
DEVOR	Stella E., 1888	16
DEVOR	Straub M., 1882	17
DEVOR	Tersey E., 1891	16
DEVOR	Thomas, 1936	80
DEVOR	Thompson White	14
DEVOR	Thompson White, 1828	16
DEVOR	Tirzah A., 1857	94
DEVOR	Velma Jean	59
DEVOR	Verda B., 1891	17
DEVOR	Victor	59
DEVOR	Victoria V., 1843	19
DEVOR	Victoria, 1867	20
DEVOR	Virgil Wayne	54
DEVOR	Virgil Wayne, 1915	59
DEVOR	Vivian, 1922	53
DEVOR	Walter Doras	71
DEVOR	Walter Doras, 1906	77
DEVOR	William Eugene Henderson, 1894	96
DEVOR	William J. Bruce, 1888	68
DEVOR	William R. 1864	20
DEVOR	William T. A., 1887	17
DEVOR	William Thompson	15
DEVOR	William Thompson, 1866	16
DEVOR	William, 1898	24
DEVOR	William, aft. 1813	12
DEVOR	Willliam J., 1856	23
DEVOR	Zella Ruth	54

INDEX

Family Name	Given Name, Birth Date	Pages
DEVOR	Zella Ruth, 1907	57
DICKINSON	Owen	80
DICKINSON	Richard D. "Dick"	61
DICKINSON	Richard Duane "Rick" 1969	61
DOWNS	Edgar	15
DOWNS	Harry	15
DOWNS	Helen	15
DOYLE	Catherine Blanch	38
DUGAS	Joe, 1942	44
DUNKLE	Eliza, 1806	11
DURYEA	Ted	52
DYKE	Henry	110
DYKE	Mary	110
DYKE	Peter	110
DYKE	Peter, Jr.	110
DYKE	Sarah	110
ELIAS	Ellen Frances	102
ELLIS	Donna, 1952	33
EPPERSON	Alice Noyes	59
ERICKSON	Stephanie	59
ERICKSON	Steve	59
ESHELMAN	Mary	16
EVITTS	Joseph	5
FAGAN	Albert Day	12
FAGAN	Anna	11
FAGAN	Barnabas, 1782	11
FAGAN	Eliza Blanche	11
FAGAN	Elizabeth Hannah	11
FAGAN	Ellen	11
FAGAN	Ethel Sarah, 1894	12
FAGAN	Hannah	11
FAGAN	Hazel Florence	12
FAGAN	James	11
FAGAN	John	11
FAGAN	Joseph Devor	11
FAGAN	Laura	12
FAGAN	Lawrence W.	12
FAGAN	Mac Kintire 1871	12
FAGAN	Mac Kintire Thomas	11
FAGAN	Maria	11
FAGAN	Martha D.	11

INDEX

Family Name	Given Name, Birth Date	Pages
FAGAN	Mary "Molly", 1870	47
FAGAN	Mary Ann	11
FAGAN	Mary E.	11
FAGAN	Merando G.	12
FAGAN	Merl S.	12
FAGAN	Nancy Elinor	11
FAGAN	Nancy Jane	11
FAGAN	Ruben L.	12
FAGAN	Ruth E.	12
FAGAN	Solomon Dunkle	11
FAGAN	Thelma F.	12
FAGAN	Theodore M.	12
FAGAN	Thomas John	11
FAGAN	Thomas John, Jr.	11
FAGAN	Ulysses	12
FAGAN	Willema	12
FAGAN	William Penn	11
FAUST	Margaret, 1833	22
FEDELEM	Katalina	78
FINK	Laura	36
FINNEY	Lulu L.	68
FLICK	Susanna, 1875	12
FLOCK (FLECK)	Rebecca, 1801	21
FORRESTER	Donald Lee	58
FORRESTER	Donald Lee, 1934	61
FORRESTER	Kimberlie Kameia, 1993	64
FORRESTER	Lisa Gay	61
FORRESTER	Mr.	57
FORRESTER	Rene Arley, 1931	58
FORRESTER	Russell Newton, 1907	57
FORRESTER	Scott Alan	61
FORRESTER	Scott Alan, 1961	63
FOUST	Emma C., 1857	23
FOX	Earl	16
FOX	L. B.	16
FOX	Stella	16
FRENCH	Alice	30
FRENCH	Amy	30
FRENCH	Amy	29
FRENCH	Bessie	30
FRENCH	Charlotte	30

INDEX

Family Name	Given Name, Birth Date	Pages
FRENCH	David, 1841/42	29
FRENCH	Elizabeth "Lizzie"	29
FRENCH	Elizabeth "Lizzie" 1867	30
FRENCH	George	30
FRENCH	James	29
FRENCH	James A.	29
FRENCH	Jemima Jane	29
FRENCH	Joseph, 1842	29
FRENCH	Lucinda	29
FRENCH	Margaret	29, 73
FRENCH	Margaret, 1848	30
FRENCH	Mary	29
FRENCH	Melvina	29
FRENCH	Melvina, 1846	30
FRENCH	Miriam Grace	29
FRENCH	Myrtle	30
FRENCH	Nancy, 1828	13
FRENCH	Robert, 1832	13
FRENCH	Sadie	30
FRENCH	Simon, 1837	13
FRENCH	Solomon, 1829	13
FRENCH	Ulysses G.	30
FRENCH	William	13, 29
FRENCH	William, 1844	29
FRENCH	William, Jr., 1836	13
FREY	Nancy	45
FRIES	Charles Alfred, 1912	39
FRYMYER	Watson	37
GALPIN	Devor Jean	81
GALPIN	Devor Jean, 1941	89
GALPIN	Eugene Charles "Gene", 1903	81
GAMBLE	David	34
GARDINER	Nina, 1901	41
GIERLICH	Suzanne	59
GILL	Amos	6
GILL	Emma	6
GILL	Willliam	6
GILMORE	Abraham "Abe" Lyons	49
GILMORE	Blanche	49
GILMORE	David	49
GILMORE	Fay	49

INDEX

Family Name	Given Name, Birth Date	Pages
GILMORE	Floyd	49
GILMORE	Guy	49
GILMORE	Jody, 1975	63
GILMORE	Julia	49
GILMORE	Maude	49
GILMORE	Maude, 1878	53
GILMORE	Pearl	49
GILMORE	Rachel	49
GILMORE	Rhoda Ann "Rhodie"	49
GLANDER	David	64
GLANDER	Luke, 1989	64
GOBEN	Helen	61
GORDON	Dorothy T., 1909	77
GOSHORN	Rev. Chalmers	72
GOULD	Renee	61
GRAHAM	Catherine, 1841	26
GRAHAM	Daniel Reid	25
GRAHAM	David, 1843	26
GRAHAM	Elizabeth, 1838	26
GRAHAM	James	26
GRAHAM	John	23, 26
GRAHAM	John, 1850	26
GRAHAM	Margaret, 1848	26
GRAHAM	Mary J., 1840	26
GRAHAM	Nancy Ann	26
GRAHAM	Nancy Ann 1831	23
GRAHAM	Reid	25
GRAHAM	Robert	5
GRAHAM	Roles, 1844	26
GRAHAM	Sarah, 1853	26
GRAHAM	William, 1834	26
GREEN	Susana	100
GREGGS	Lucille, 1924	88
GROCE	Irene	38
GROSVENOR	Dorothy Jean	85
GROSVENOR	Dorothy Jean, 1945	89
GROSVENOR	Fred Browne, M.D.	83
GROSVENOR	Richard Browne, 1916	83
GROSVENOR	Susan Mae, 1950	85
GROVE	Sadie E., 1865	109
GROVENBURG	Ward	52

INDEX

Family Name	Given Name, Birth Date	Pages
GURY	Anna	38
GURY	Francis	38
GURY	Jay	38
GURY	William J.	38
HACKARD	Fred	25
HACKARD	Helen, 1923	25
HAINES	Sarah Ann	69
HALL	Mr. & Mrs Orin	93
HALL	Rebecca Jane	73
HALL	Richard Eugene	93
HALL	Stanley Loren, 1944	90
HALSTEAD	Andrew	53
HAMBLEY	Alan Ward	90
HAMBLEY	Alan Ward, 1971	94
HAMBLEY	Brooke Ariel, 1992	94
HAMBLEY	Gloria Kay	90
HAMBLEY	Gloria Kay, 1968	93
HAMBLEY	Harold Ward "Bud"	90
HAMBLEY	Katelynn Marie, 1993	94
HAMBLEY	Kathryn Eileen "Kathy"	90
HAMBLEY	Kathryn Eileen "Kathy", 1962	93
HAMBLEY	Kimberly Ann "Kim"	90
HAMBLEY	Kimberly Ann "Kim", 1964	93
HAMBLEY	Kristina "Tina" Lynn	90
HAMBLEY	Kristina "Tina" Lynn, 1966	93
HAMBLEY	Lester A.	90
HAMILTON	Clarence	58
HAMMING	Rosalie	43
HAMMOND	Alice Ida	31
HAMMOND	Alice Ida, 1858	69
HAMMOND	George Washington Shearer	33
HAMMOND	Jacob	69
HAMMOND	Lavina Mae	33
HAMMOND	Margaret, 1839	34
HAMMOND	Maria "Jennie" Jane	29
HAMMOND	Martin Lawrence	69
HAMMOND	Martin Philip	69
HAMMOND	Philip	34, 69
HARDY	Catherine M.	24
HARRIS	Hallie May	57
HARTZELL	Annie	102

INDEX

Family Name	Given Name, Birth Date	Pages
HASHINGER	Adam	94
HAUSEN	Robert E.	42
HAWLEY	Anna May	75
HAWLEY	Anna May, 1917	83
HAWLEY	Betty Lois	76
HAWLEY	Betty Lois, 1921	87
HAWLEY	Carolyn Kay, 1969	91
HAWLEY	Carrie	6
HAWLEY,	Henry Allen	73
HAWLEY	James Henry, 1942	87
HAWLEY	Janice Eileen	87
HAWLEY	Janice Eileen, 1943	90
HAWLEY,	Miller Henry, 1884	73
HAWLEY	Nora Grace	70
HAWLEY	Nora Grace, 1920	75
HAWLEY	Ray Allen	75
HAWLEY	Ray Allen, 1918	86
HAWLEY	Robert Ray	87
HAWLEY	Robert Ray, 1946	91
HAWLEY	Robert Richard "Robbie", 1973	91
HAWLEY	Stephanie Arlene, 1971	91
HAYDEN	John	66
HAYNES	Daniel W.	65
HAZENFELT	Lydia	17
HEATON	A. C. S.	108
HEATON	Carrie	99
HEATON	Charles	99
HEATON	Collins	99
HEATON	Daniel	99
HEATON	Emma	99
HEATON	Eugene	108
HEATON	George	108
HEATON	Georgia	99
HEATON	Gus	99
HEATON	Hariett	99
HEATON	Harvey	108
HEATON	James	99
HEATON	Mollie	99
HEATON	Will	99
HEIDEMAN	Fred	66
HEIM	Britt May	63

INDEX

Family Name	Given Name, Birth Date	Pages
HEIM	Craig	63
HEMINGER	Fay	25
HENRY	Andrea Gail, 1956	43
HENRY	Ellen	101
HENRY	James Robert, 1947	43
HENRY	Jill Kathleen, 1963	43
HENRY	Myra	102
HENRY	Paula Jean, 1957	43
HENRY	Robert B., 1926	43
HENSCHEL	Brandon Kai, 1991	93
HENSCHEL	Werner G. "Verne"	93
HIGANBOTHAN	Sarah	49
HILLIARD	Sarah A.	25
HOCKENBERRY	Carolyn	45
HOLANDBAUGH	Darlene, 1946	92
HOLLAND	Elizabeth	100
HOLLAND	Hannah	100
HOLLINGSWORTH	Elizabeth	3
HOLLINGSWORTH	Jesse	3
HOLLINGSWORTH	Joseph	3
HOLLINGSWORTH	Robert	3
HOOD	Sarah	88
HOSSLER	Mary Ann, 1830	14
HOUCK	Eva	65
HOUCK	Mary 1812	7
HOUSEMAN	Miss	103
HOUSEMAN	Elizabeth (REFFLE), 1947	91
HURST	Evelyn	37
HURST	John Kuezer	37
HUTCHINSON	Helen C.	45
JAMESON	Ruth, 1948	88
JENNINGS	Albert Knapp "Hal"	54
JENNINGS	Beth	55, 59
JENNINGS	Chuck	59
JENNINGS	Ellen	55
JENNINGS	Kenneth	55, 59
JENSEN	Martin L.	67
JESSIE	Charlotte Elizabeth	57
JOHNSON	Alex Wayne Sather, 1988	64
JOHNSON	Brandon, 1991	93
JOHNSON	Corali, 1906	63

INDEX

Family Name	Given Name, Birth Date	Pages
JOHNSON	Cristen, 1990	93
JOHNSON	Daniel Scott, 1987	93
JOHNSON	Donald Wayne, 1972	62
JOHNSON	Edwin	59
JOHNSON	Jody Carrol, 1971	62, 64
JOHNSON	Oliver Cecil, 1916	59
JOHNSON	Richard Sather, 1989	64
JOHNSON	Ronald Sather, 1987	64
JOHNSON	Steven Michael	60, 63
JOHNSON	Vivian Kay	60, 62
JOHNSON	Wayne Carrol	60
JOHNSON	Wayne Carrol, 1945	62
JOHNSON	Wesley "Wes"	93
JOHNSTON	Arthur A. 1866	71
JOHNSTON	Edith Catherine "Edie Kay", 1918	82
JOHNSTON	Jay Corwin	71, 81
JOHNSTON	Lester Wendell, 1893	71
JOHNSTON	Quentin	53
JOHNSTON	Robert, 1912	82
JOHNSTON	Samuel A	71, 72, 82
JONES	Ed G.	24
JONES	Rena Kay, 1960	44
JONES	Robert Wesley	24
KALTENBAUGH	Allen	77
KALTENBAUGH	Allen, 1923	88
KALTENBAUGH	Bruce	77
KALTENBAUGH	Bruce Allen	88
KALTENBAUGH	Bruce Allen, 1944	92
KALTENBAUGH	Frank Howard	76
KALTENBAUGH	Gayle, 1967	92
KALTENBAUGH	Jill, 1970	92
KALTENBAUGH	John	76
KALTENBAUGH	Leslie Dean	88
KALTENBAUGH	Leslie Dean, 1946	92
KALTENBAUGH	Stacy, 1969	92
KALTENBAUGH	Tracey, 1966	92
KECKLER	Rachel, 1832	16
KEENE	Jim. 1942	63
KEN	Michail	8
KENNEDY	James "Jim" Findley, 1949	85
KERLIN	Phoebe, 1879	101

INDEX

Family Name	Given Name, Birth Date	Pages
KING	Irline	59
KING	Nancy Elizabeth, 1847	107
KIRKPATRICK	Amos McGinley, 1851	69
KIRKPATRICK	Jacob McGinley	69
KIRKPATRICK	Lacea Dorcas	69
KIRKPATRICK	Lodemma	69
KIRKPATRICK	Luetta	69
KITAJCHUK	Laura	61, 63
KITAJCHUK	Marla	61, 63
KITAJCHUK	Marlene	61
KITAJCHUK	Valerie	61, 63
KITZMILLER	Nancy, 1952	43
KLING	Charles	35
KLING	Elisha	35
KLING	Elizabeth	35
KLING	George	35
KLING	Henry,	35
KLING	Jane	35
KLING	Jesse	35
KLING	Margaret	35
KLING	Martha	35
KLING	Robert	35
KNIGHT	Ronald R.	42
KORN	Billy	55
KREPTS	Albert	102
KRIST	William	102
KUHN	Mary	35
KURTZ	Greta	37
KURTZ	Mary	37
KURTZ	Ralph A.	37
KURTZ	Raymond	37
LAIDIG	Andrew	109
LAIDIG	Edward Arlington, 1878	109
LAIDIG	Elsie Dell Ray, 1884	109
LAIDIG	Mary E.	105
LAIDIG	Michael, 1852	109
LAIRD	Mary Ann	48
LAMBERSON	Daniel	105
LAMBERSON	Elizabeth	105
LAMBERSON	Ellen	105
LAMBERSON	Jacob	105

INDEX

Family Name	Given Name, Birth Date	Pages
LAMBERSON	Samuel	105
LANDIS	Larry	45
LANTHERS	Samuel	94
LAUSHEY	Clara	40
LAUTHERS	J. Ray, 1905	47
LAUTHERS	Roger J., 1939	47
LAUVER	Douglas Brent, 1957	43
LEAVITT	Arthur	18
LEAVITT	Carrie	18
LEAVITT	Dwight S	18
LEAVITT	Newman	18
LEMAZZI	Betty Lou	61
LIGHTNER	Charles S.,1880	73
LIGHTNER	Jessie Cromwell	73
LIGHTNER	Jessie Cromwell, 1924	82
LIGHTNER	John H	73
LINN	Carrie	72
LINN	Lulu	101
LONG	Bathsheba	13
LONG	Fred	13
LONG	Mary Virginia	13
LOVE	Elaine	41
LOVE	Freeburn Paul	41
LOVE	Grace Beryl. 1892	32
LOVE	Grace Beryl	31
LOVE	Howard, 1863	30
LOVE	Marlene	41
LOVE	Norman	41
LUSK	Cornelia, 1836	20
MACHAL	Edward	46
MACHAL	George Edward	46
MACHAL	Nina Marie, 1958	46
MALMGREN	April Linnea, 1986	33
MALMGREN	Jeffren Nels, 1981	33
MALMGREN	Karena Noelle, 1987	34
MALMGREN	Paul David, 1951	33
MASON	Amber	61
MASON	Erin	61
MASON	Louis, 1939	59
MASON	Paul	59
MASON	Rex	59

INDEX

Family Name	Given Name, Birth Date	Pages
MASON	Rex, 1947	61
MATTINGLY	Fannie	20
MENDENHALL	Frank	52
MERRIFIELD	Frances	19
MERRIFIELD	Hubert	19
MERRIFIELD	L. L.	19
MILES	(_____)	52
MILES	Clarence	52
MILLER	Ada	95
MILLER	Ann Margaret, 1911	42
MILLER	Catherine	8
MILLER	Elizabeth	104
MILLER	Faye	53
MILLER	George S.	21
MILLER	Jacob	8
MITCHELL	Jodi	94
MORRIS	Avis Darlene, 1927	25
MORRIS	Donald Eugene, 1923	25
MORRIS	Leslie Edward, 1928	25
MORRIS	Melvin Ernest	24
MORRIS	Riley	25
MORRIS	Rolland "Darrell", 1925	25
MORROW	Ann	12
McCLAIN	Alfred	14
McCLAIN	Annie	14
McCLAIN	J. Allen	14
McCLAIN	James	30
McCLAIN	Jane	14
McCLAIN	Mary Elizabeth, 1866	37
McCLAIN	Sarah "Sadie", 1881	30
McCLAIN	Theodore	14
McDOWELL	Laura Belle, 1860	109
McILROY	Joseph "Joe"	72
McKEAN	Margaret Jane	103
McKIBBEN	Matilda	18
McLAINE	Hazel	107
McLAINE	William C., 1853	107
McMULLEN	Mary McElhaney. 1899	40
NAFTSGAR	David	16
NEAL	Amy	8
NEAL	David	7, 8

INDEX

Family Name	Given Name, Birth Date	Pages
NEAL	Elizabeth	8
NEAL	Esther	8
NEAL	Henry	7
NEAL	Mary	8
NEAL	Mary Louise	25
NEAL	Nancy	8
NEAL	Ruth	8
NEAL	William	8
NEIL	Susannah	31
NEILSON	Tammy, 1963	63
NEISWANDER	(____)	29
NELSON	Elizabeth	72
NELSON	Esther	72, 82
NELSON	Hilda	72
NELSON	Mary	72
NELSON	Newton	72
NESBITT	Ada Mary 1878	70
NESBITT	Amos	36
NESBITT	Etna	36, 70
NESBITT	Jesse	36
NESBITT	John	36
NESBITT	John P.	36
NESBITT	Jones	36
NESBITT	Mary	36
NESBITT	Shearer	36
NESBITT	Thomas	36
NESBITT	William	36
NOLAND	Mark	61
OSTRA	Michael, 1950	44
OTT	Charles, 1928	44
OTT	Nancy Louise, 1949	44
PATRICK	Duwayne McKerrick, 1944	42
PETERSON	Alfred Shade, 1854	14
PETERSON	Almira Jane, 1846	14
PETERSON	Amanda Bell, 1855	14
PETERSON	Annie Elizabeth, 1838	14
PETERSON	David	6
PETERSON	James	6, 14
PETERSON	Mary Agnes, 1850	14
PETERSON	Melinda Jane	48
PETERSON	Robert	6

INDEX

Family Name	Given Name, Birth Date	Pages
PETERSON	Ruemma "Amy", 1815	6
PETERSON	Theodore Calvin, 1853	14
PETTIS	Lorenzo Dow "Ranny"	54
PETTIS	Maude Mabel, 1885	54
PHILLIPS	Brandon	63
PHILLIPS	Bret	63
PHILLIPS	Jenai	63
PIERCE	Merle	51
PILES	Hannah, 1799	7
PLUEBELL	Bessie	39
PLUEBELL	David	40
PLUEBELL	Edwin	40
PLUEBELL	Given	39
PLUEBELL	Jack, 1878	39
PLUEBELL	John	39
PLUEBELL	Kenneth	39
PLUEBELL	Raymond	40
PLUEBELL	Robert	40
PLUEBELL	Thelma	39
PLUEBELL	William	39
POTTER	Joseph	102
POTTER	Richard	52
PRICE	Kenneth Marion	87
PRICE	Sandra Kay, 1943	87
PRITCHARD	Edith	20
PRITCHARD	Mildred	20
PRITCHARD	Thomas	19
RAMSEY	Clara	101
REED	Sadie, 1887	81
REFFLE	Elizabeth, 1947	91
REFFLE	Josef	91
RERICK	Carl	18
RERICK	John	18
RERICK	John H., M.D.	18
RERICK	Rolland	18
RHINE	Margaret	7
RHINEHART	George L.	44
RHINEHART	George, 1922	44
RHOADS	Harriet G.	103
RICE	Nancy L., 1943	44
RICHARDSON	Mabel	30

INDEX

Family Name	Given Name, Birth Date	Pages
RICHARDSON	William	30
ROBERSON	Blanche	62
ROBERSON	Gerald Clair, 1936	62
ROBERSON	Keerah Yvonne, 1990	64
ROBERSON	Kimberly Dawn, 1967	62, 64
ROBERSON	Michael Scott, 1965	62
ROBERSON	Richard Wayne, 1968	62, 64
ROBINSON	(____)	4
ROBINSON	Charles	100
ROBINSON	Dorothy, 1925	43
ROBINSON	Homer	100
ROBINSON	Ivey	100
ROBINSON	John	100
ROBINSON	Lillian	100
ROBINSON	Maude	100
ROBINSON	Merrill	100
ROBINSON	Nettie	96
ROBINSON	William	100
RODGERS	Harrison Lang	42
RODGERS	Judith Ann	42
RODGERS	Sharyn Lang	42
RODGERS	Timothy Lang	42
ROLES-RAGAN	Sarah Ellen	3, 4
ROLES	John	5
ROLES	Lydia	5
ROLLINS	Mary Ann, 1926	96
ROSE	Elias	14
ROWLAND,	Linette, 1860	17
RUCKER	Hazel May	90
RUSSELL	Catherine "Kate"	50
RUTHERFORD	Sarah A., 1827	102
SALKIELD	Albert	104
SALKIELD	Alice	104
SALKIELD	Franklin	104
SALKIELD	Hannah	104
SALKIELD	Jacob F	104
SALKIELD	John	104
SALKIELD	Samuel Wesley, 1839	104
SALKIELD	Sarah	104
SANNO	John	29
SEIGFRIED	Joan	40

INDEX

Family Name	Given Name, Birth Date	Pages
SHAFER	John	101
SHARP	Eleanor Bernice	35
SHAW	Mary Jane, 1884	52
SHEARER	Alan Clair	44
SHEARER	Alan Claire, 1959	46
SHEARER	Alma Hope, 1897	39
SHEARER	Amos	34
SHEARER	Amos Harold, 1902	38
SHEARER	Amos, 1838	34
SHEARER	Andrew B., 1963	45
SHEARER	Anna Creigh, 1892	38
SHEARER	Anna M., 1876	35
SHEARER	Anna Mae	41
SHEARER	Anna Mae, 1928	44
SHEARER	Bert Doyle 1909	38
SHEARER	Bessie Mae	35
SHEARER	Bessie Mae, 1880	39
SHEARER	Betsy Jo, 1962	45
SHEARER	Betty June	40, 43
SHEARER	Carolyn	40
SHEARER	Clair Lorraine	41
SHEARER	Clair Lorraine, 1925	43
SHEARER	Clair McClain	40
SHEARER	Clara	36
SHEARER	Clark	36
SHEARER	David	34, 36
SHEARER	David Henry	35
SHEARER	David Henry, 1869	38
SHEARER	Doris Jean	41
SHEARER	Doris Jean, 1929	45
SHEARER	Dorothy Mae, 1903	38
SHEARER	Earl James	39
SHEARER	Earl James, 1902	42
SHEARER	Edna, 1889	37
SHEARER	Edward	45
SHEARER	Elizabeth May, 1907	39
SHEARER	Ellen	36
SHEARER	Emma	34, 36
SHEARER	Emma Mildred	38
SHEARER	Ethel May, 1888	37
SHEARER	Frank	36

INDEX

Family Name	Given Name, Birth Date	Pages
SHEARER	Frederick Carl	38
SHEARER	Frederick Carl, 1900	41
SHEARER	Frederick Clair McClain	37, 40
SHEARER	Garry James, 1951	43
SHEARER	Gloria	42
SHEARER	Gloria, 1939	46
SHEARER	Gordon S	40, 43
SHEARER	Grace	36
SHEARER	Hannah	35
SHEARER	Harold, 1922	41
SHEARER	Harvey Donald	39
SHEARER	Harvey Donald, 1901	41
SHEARER	Harvey Donald, III, 1956	45
SHEARER	Harvey Donald, Jr	41
SHEARER	Harvey Donald, Jr., 1931	45
SHEARER	Heidi Diane, 1980	46
SHEARER	Helen Elizabeth, 1879	37
SHEARER	Henry, 1816	34
SHEARER	Herbert West, 1904	37
SHEARER	Ida Margarita, 1910	39
SHEARER	Ida	36
SHEARER	Jane	34, 35
SHEARER	Jeffrey Nathaniel, 1961	44
SHEARER	Jeffrey Weary	45
SHEARER	Jeffrey Weary, 1959	47
SHEARER	Jennie	36
SHEARER	Jennifer Lee	43
SHEARER	Jesse	34, 36
SHEARER	John	36
SHEARER	John Alfred, 1873	35
SHEARER	John S., 1902	37
SHEARER	Jonathan	34, 35
SHEARER	Karl Alexander, 1896	37
SHEARER	Kenneth Lee	42
SHEARER	Kimberly Ann, 1975	46
SHEARER	Leroy	39
SHEARER	Leroy, 1899	41
SHEARER	Lillian, 1895	39
SHEARER	Linda	42
SHEARER	Lois Annalee, 1931	41
SHEARER	Lois Elaine	42

INDEX

Family Name	Given Name, Birth Date	Pages

Family Name	Given Name, Birth Date	Pages
SHEARER	Lois Elaine, 1938	46
SHEARER	Lola Vernal, 1893	38
SHEARER	Lori Jo, 1960	44
SHEARER	Louise Margaret, 1917	40
SHEARER	Lyman	36
SHEARER	Lyman Bruce	38
SHEARER	Lyman Bruce, 1896	40
SHEARER	Martha Ann	35
SHEARER	Margaret	36
SHEARER	Margaret Ann, 1941	42
SHEARER	Marjorie Catherine	41
SHEARER	Marjorie Catherine, 1921	43
SHEARER	Martha, 1930	41
SHEARER	Mary	35, 36
SHEARER	Mary Catherine, 1907	37
SHEARER	Mary Susan	35
SHEARER	Mathew Curtis, 1971	44
SHEARER	Mathew Scott, 1981	47
SHEARER	Maude	36
SHEARER	Michael	34, 36
SHEARER	Michael J., 1878	35
SHEARER	Miriam Mae, 1919	41
SHEARER	Monte Clair	37
SHEARER	Monte Clair, 1898	40
SHEARER	Neidi Jo, 1967	45
SHEARER	Paul	36
SHEARER	Philip West	35
SHEARER	Philip West, 1866	37
SHEARER	Raymond Dwight	37
SHEARER	Raymond Dwight, 1895	40
SHEARER	Richard Darwin	41, 44
SHEARER	Richard Lee	42
SHEARER	Richard Lee, 1934	45
SHEARER	Richard Todd, 1962	44
SHEARER	Robert	45
SHEARER	Romain Carl, 1905	39
SHEARER	Rosalyn	41
SHEARER	Rosalyn, 1922	44
SHEARER	Ruth	36, 40
SHEARER	Ruth Margaret, 1893	37
SHEARER	Ruth, 1919	42

INDEX

Family Name	Given Name, Birth Date	Pages

Family Name	Given Name, Birth Date	Pages
SHEARER	Stephanie	43
SHEARER	Susan Lynn, 1958	45
SHEARER	Teresa Ida, 1862	35
SHEARER	Tracey Ann, 1960	45
SHEARER	Twila Dawn, 1943	46
SHEARER	Twila Dawn	42
SHEARER	Valerie Jo Anne, 1969	45
SHEARER	Wendy Nanette, 1965	44
SHEARER	William	8,34,36
SHEARER	William Harvey	35
SHEARER	William Harvey, 1871	38
SHEARER	William Linden	42
SHEARER	William Linden, 1933	45
SHEARER	William Linden, Jr., 1957	45
SHEARER	William West, 1906	38
SHERRER	Barbara, 1952	82
SHERRER	Gene	82
SHERRER	Robert, 1948	82
SHETLER	Maria	47
SHOEMAKER	Edna	46
SHOOP	Bonnie	41
SHOOP	Carol	41
SHOOP	Irwin Snively, 1916	40
SHOOP	Larry	41
SHOOP	Patricia	41
SHOOP	Ray	41
SHOPE	Lizzie	21
SHREINER	Elias	22
SHREINER	Leah, 1804	22
SHUE	Freda	72
SHULTZ	Carl	43
SHULTZ	James	35
SHULTZ	Karen Lee	43
SHULTZ	Mark Edward	43
SHULTZ	Martha Lynn	43
SHULTZ	Tod Andrew	43
SICKLES	Benjamin	15
SICKLES	Nancy, 1832	15
SINNHUBER	James	88
SIPES	Rebecca	99
SKINNER	Cora Nettie	32

INDEX

Family Name	Given Name, Birth Date	Pages
SKINNER	J. McGinley "Max", 1871	66
SMILEY	Richard Charles, 1957	43
SMITH	Ada Beatrice, 1866	95
SMITH	Harry	100
SMITH	John	95
SNARE	Mary	102
SNODGRASS	John	53
SORSETH	Alvin Lloyd "Tyke"	92
SORSETH	Craig Randall, 1947	92
SORSETH	Noah Nakai, 1996	93
SOUTHWICK	Isabel	24
SPANN	Warner	59
SPEARS	Paul Douglas, 1965	86
SPEERS	Duane	86
SPORTSMAN	Arlene Joyce	92
SPRACKLIN	Peter "Pete"	50
SPRACKLIN	Sabina Jane "Bina", 1860	50
STARR	Martha H	19
STEELE	Anna, 1902	72
STEELE	Bruce, 1904	72
STEELE	Donald, 1898	72
STEELE	Marie, 1896	72
STEELE	William Tecumseh, 1869	72
STEVENS	Albert F., M.D., 1861	101
STEVENS	Andrew, 1875	103
STEVENS	Annie M	103
STEVENS	Benjamin Edmonson	101
STEVENS	Bessie May	101
STEVENS	Carlton	101
STEVENS	Charles Escoe	102
STEVENS	Charlie, 1862	102
STEVENS	Clubine R	103
STEVENS	Edward Gray	102
STEVENS	Edward Luther, 1869	100
STEVENS	Elizabeth Alice 1862	100
STEVENS	Elizabeth S., 1860	102
STEVENS	Emma Frances, 1859	101
STEVENS	Emory Clark, 1870	100
STEVENS	Florence Lavina, 1855	100
STEVENS	Franklin K., D.D.S, 1863	102
STEVENS	George	100

INDEX

Family Name	Given Name, Birth Date	Pages
STEVENS	Hannah Elizabeth	101
STEVENS	Hannah, 1814	104
STEVENS	Hester Olive	101
STEVENS	Ida M., 1864	102
STEVENS	Isaac	101
STEVENS	Jacob Taylor	99
STEVENS	Jacob Taylor, 1829	102
STEVENS	James Dyke	101
STEVENS	James Lane, 1824	99
STEVENS	James Lane	99
STEVENS	James Vincent, 1848	100
STEVENS	John C.	103
STEVENS	John F., M.D., 1855	101
STEVENS	John Scott	100
STEVENS	John Wesley	99
STEVENS	John Wesley, 1839	103
STEVENS	Joseph Deavor	99,102
STEVENS	Joseph Deavor, 1827	100
STEVENS	Juniata Amanda, 1853	100
STEVENS	Lemuel Green, 1859	100
STEVENS	Lillie Belle, 1890	103
STEVENS	Margaret, 1855	102
STEVENS	Marion, 1877	103
STEVENS	Martha Belle, 1866	100
STEVENS	Martha M., 1837	99
STEVENS	Mary E., 1853	102
STEVENS	Mary J.	99
STEVENS	Mary Jane, 1850	100
STEVENS	Mary Ray	101
STEVENS	Mertie Emma	101
STEVENS	Missouri	100
STEVENS	Nathan H.	101
STEVENS	Nellie B.	103
STEVENS	Nellie Belle	101
STEVENS	Olive	100
STEVENS	Philip Deavor, 1826	100
STEVENS	Philip Deavor	99
STEVENS	Rebecca V., 1851	102
STEVENS	Rev. Benjamin Fletcher	99
STEVENS	Rev. Benjamin Fletcher, 1831	103
STEVENS	Rev. George Washington, 1857	101

INDEX

Family Name	Given Name, Birth Date	Pages
STEVENS	Rev. I. C.	99
STEVENS	Samuel, 1867	102
STEVENS	Sarah Alberda	101
STEVENS	Theodore Taylor, 1863	100
STEVENS	Thomas B., 1839	100
STEVENS	Vincent C., 1852	101
STEVENS	Vincent, 1797	99
STEVENS	Vincent, 1875	103
STEVENS	William	100
STEVENS	William F.	103
STEVENS	William T., 1857	102
STILES	Sue Lease, 1954	43
STITT	J. D.	69
STITT	Ruth Barclay	33
STORTZ	Irene	53
STOTLER	Sue, 1849	108
STRUNK	Catherine Ann	25
STUDER	Pauline	88
SWAN	Emma	14
SWAN	Ora	35
SWARTZ	Mary	43
SWICKARD	Olive Evangeline	83
SWOPE	Jacob G.	21
TAKACH	Joseph "Joe"	78
TAKACH	Mary	6
TAKACH	Mary Ann, 1914	78
TALLMAN	John Blaine	49
TALLMAN	Lulu	49
TALLMAN	Mae	49
TANERI	Tery	92
TAYLOR	Charles	89
TAYLOR	Mary Ann Elizabeth	5
TAYLOR	Mrs. William, Jr.	89
TAYLOR	Nettie	15
TAYLOR	Richard "Dick" L., 1936	89
TAYLOR	Robert	89
TAYLOR	Robin Irene, 1977	89
TAYLOR	Sarah Jane	89
TAYLOR	Violet Ann, 1975	89
TAYLOR	William	89
TAYLOR	William Barclay, Sr.	89

INDEX

Family Name	Given Name, Birth Date	Pages
TELSHAW	Lucy	61
THATCHER	Evelyn, 1902	41
THIENES	Ethel	59
THIESSEN	Lucy I.	90
THOMAS	Barbara	91
THOMAS	Milo	15
THOMPSON	Ann	13
THOMPSON	Ruth	59
TICE	Herbert "Herb"	32
TICE	Margaret "Peg"	32
TICE	Ruth	32
TOLLIVER	C. R.	16
TOTTEN	Katie, 1871	110
ULRICH	John	37
ULRICH	Nancy	37
ULRICH	Ralph	37
VAN HOUTON	Edward J.	62
VENABLE	Marc Jeffrey	93
WAGNER	Harrison	21
WALKER	Charles Devor, 1889	68
WALKER	Ira Jacob	68
WALKER	Jesse Winfield, 1882	68
WALKER	John Brinley, 1887	68
WALKER	Mary Lydica	68
WALKER	Mary Lydica, 1875	72
WALKER	Newton Hayes, 1894	68
WALKER	Nora Elizabeth, 1879	68
WALKER	Samuel Alexander, 1880	68
WALKER	Winfield Andrew, 1850	67
WALKER	Zeola Belle	68
WALKER	Zeola Belle, 1885	73
WALTERS	Beverly	40
WALTERS	James	40
WALTERS	Jay R.	40
WALTERS	John	40
WANDER	George	8
WARREN,	Melinda Sue, 1956	45
WARREN,	Richard Paul	45
WARRINGTON	Miranda Ellen	54
WEARIN	Everett, 1897	55
WEARIN	James Everett	56

INDEX

Family Name	Given Name, Birth Date	Pages
WEARIN	James Everett, 1926	60
WEARIN	Jamie Everett	61
WEARIN	Jamie Everett, 1956	63
WEARIN	Jason, 1976	63
WEARIN	Joy, 1978	63
WEARIN	Lilah	56
WEARIN	Lilah, 1924	59
WEARIN	M. J.	55
WEARIN	Mindy	63
WEARIN	Shannon Lee	61
WEARIN	Shannon Lee, 1942	63
WEARY	Jo Ann M.	45
WEBBER	Terry Elizabeth	47
WEBER	Margaret Matilda	76
WEIR	Anna Frances, 1921	86
WEIR	James Summerville	86
WERT	Constance	41
WERT	Sallie	41
WERT	Susan	41
WERT	William Solomon, 1934	41
WHITE	Sally	78, 79
WIBLE	Frank	69
WIKER	Mabel	40
WILKLOW	Sarah	53
WILLET	Samuel	21
WILLIAMS	Jack Lee, 1940	89
WILLIAMS	Jody Kay, 1964	46
WILLIAMS	Renee Yvonne	90
WILLIAMS	Renee Yvonne, 1964	92
WILLIAMS	Richard Alan, 1960	46
WILLIAMS	Richard Ellis	46
WILLIAMS	Vickie Mae, 1962	46
WILSON	David	31 58
WILSON	Faye	31
WILSON	Hazel, 1902	31
WILSON	Isaac	31
WILSON	James	31
WILSON	Kathleen	31
WILSON	Mathew Cowan	32
WILSON	Melvina Eliza Narcessa	32
WILSON	Norman	31

INDEX

Family Name	Given Name, Birth Date	Pages
WILSON	Thelma, 1903	31
WILSON	Warren, 1908	31
WILSON	Wesley	31
WILTZ	Albert	53
WINTERS	Donald	46
WINTERS	Jacob	46
WINTERS	Joyann	46
WOLVINGTON	(_____)	49
WOODS	Melva	62
WOODY	Charles	49
WOODY	Reuben	49
WORK	Mariah Lettice	67
WRIGHT	Gertrude C.	101
YINGLING	Angeline, 1822	106
YINGLING	Peter	106